SOPHIA LOREN'S
Recipes & Memories

Sophia Loren's
Recipes & Memories

By Sophia Loren

PHOTOGRAPHS
ALISON HARRIS

ART DIRECTION AND DESIGN
JOEL AVIRON

PROJECT EDITOR
CAROLE LALLI

GREMESE

Preceding page: With my mother, just after the end of the Second World War

PHOTO CREDITS
Kobal: *page 11, top*: CCC/Concordia; *page 11, bottom*: AVCO Embassy;
page 35: CCC/Canafox; *page 59*: Reteitalia; *page 81*: Paramount;
page 122: Twentieth Century Fox; *page 149*: Titanus Societe Generale;
page 200: CCC Filmkunst
Corbis-Bettman: *page 34, 56*: John Springer

TRANSLATION: CAROL AMORUSO

COPYEDITOR/PROOFREADER: LIANA FREDLEY AND ALEXEI COHEN

FOOD STYLING: MARIANN SAUVION

PROP STYLING: CECI GALLINI

DESIGN ASSISTANTS: JASON SNYDER AND MEGHAN DAY HEALEY

We would like to thank RICHARD GINORI for his kind assistance.

First published in 1998 by GT Publishing Corporation
New Soft Covered Edition
GREMESE 2005 © E.G.E. s.r.l.
Via Virginia Agnelli, 88 – 00151 Rome (Italy)

ISBN: 88-7301-582-4

Printed in Italy

This book is dedicated to my grandmother, Nonna Luisa,
not only for the many things I've learned from her,
but for her ability to transform even the most ordinary food
into something delectable.

I was thrilled to win my Oscar for Two Women. *Cary Grant called me in the middle of the night in Rome with the good news— I had been far too nervous to go to Hollywood.*

FOREWORD

*T*his is how it happened. A new edition of the popular book *Sophia Loren's Memories & Recipes* was being prepared and the publisher asked me if I'd write a few lines of introduction. Out of friendship and affection for the author, the extraordinary Sophia Loren, I did not hesitate to take up my pen. I was even a little curious.

For here is an occasion to read all the tried and tested recipes of someone you wouldn't expect to find in the kitchen draining pasta. But Sophia is there and tells all about her childhood recollections of Pozzuoli, near Naples in Italy, of the first time she tasted caviar and when she discovered macaroni *Carbonara* while filming *La Ciocara* on the Apennine mountains, in central Italy. It all seems so very normal. Everything she touches appears to shine and becomes special. Her recipes, even the simplest ones, have an unusual quality, a rich flavour, they contain the liveliness and zest of genuine Italy. Like Sophia herself.

For someone like me who loves food but is certainly not an aspiring chef who enjoys the company of pots and pans, I think it would be entertaining to open this book on evenings with friends and say: "So what's it going to be tonight? The lemon spaghetti or the potato croquettes?" I'm sure, with her advice, I'd succeed in becoming a great cook. Who knows, she may even write about it in her next book...

Giorgio Armani

CONTENTS

Introduction xi

*Antipasti
and Small Dishes* 3

Soup 29

Pasta 47

Rice & Polenta 79

Meat 97

Fish 129

Vegetables 151

Desserts 183

INDEX 203

INTRODUCTION

According to an old Italian adage, the best condiment for any food is hunger. No delicacies or frills can make food as appetizing as an empty belly can. Those of us who were children during the Second World War can bear prime witness to this great truth. Hunger—real, visceral hunger—forced us to face many dangers in those years, but it also gave us great courage, and even today I remain in awe of what we experienced.

Waves of fighter planes and bombers, and almost daily explosions and crashes, greeted us just a stone's throw from my grandmother Luisa's kitchen in Pozzuoli, the small city just outside of Naples where I was born. I'd clutch Nonna Luisa's skirts while we made the sign of the cross and waited for the din to subside and leave us unharmed. It wasn't that I was particularly foolhardy or courageous, but even in the midst of the bombings I would be anticipating, with all the strength my stomach could muster, the pleasure that eating would bring. We could hear bombs exploding and the crackle of anti-aircraft guns in nearby Bagnoli, where there were factories, but my grandmother stayed in her trench, behind her battery of pots and pans, and nothing in the world would have made me miss the delicacies that she cooked up. I say

OPPOSITE: *My writing table at home in Geneva with recipes and a favorite photograph of Nonna Luisa.*
RIGHT: *First communion. I was nine years old and almost overcome by emotion—because of the impact of the day itself and because of the aerial bombing that interrupted the ceremony. One bomb fell about three hundred yards from the church.*

"delicacies" as a manner of speaking, because what we had was meager and humble. Our larder was impoverished, but with a few sprigs of fresh herbs Nonna Luisa could transform even our plain stale bread into an elegant dish.

When the war was over, flour from America began to flow into our kitchen, the Italian countryside began to bear fruit again, and culinary customs were revived; hunger was no longer the most plentiful condiment in Nonna Luisa's kitchen. But the war years had imprinted on my soul and on my sensibilities certain indelible flavors that are with me still.

It is perhaps because of those days that I feel so strongly about the family and its role as the foundation of society. For me, the family is sacred. A strong family provides the mutual love, commitment, and honesty that allow us to grow up true to ourselves and to our fellow human beings. As a mother and as a citizen of the world, I am concerned that the collapse of this social nucleus is forcing us to become anxious, fearful, and uncertain about the future.

These may be curious thoughts to introduce a cookbook, even one as personal as mine. But I want you to remember that the kitchen, its environment and its ritual, is where the whole family is united. The traditional components include a father, mother, children, even grandparents. Today some families are defined differently, but no matter its makeup, the ritual of the table is a family's strongest bond. For me, it's an irrepressible joy to think of how many secrets and doubts, how many resentments, disappointments, and negative thoughts, can find a peaceful solution at the table. Confessions, debates, advice, and resolution of the mini-tragedies that crop up in our daily lives all find their way to the table. It's a small universe of peace, the clearest proof of the ties of affection and love that exist in our little community.

Wherever I may be, I have photographs of those I love, my family and my dearest friends.

ACKNOWLEDGMENTS

This book could not exist without the inspiration of my mother, Romilda. I wish she could be beside me as I turn the pages.

My sister Maria is another of the marvelous cooks who bless our family. Maria continues to set a standard of excellence I aspire to.

For many, many years Ruth Bapst and Ines Bruscia have helped me in ways no job descriptions ever could conceive. Their assistance and support during the months of work on this book were invaluable.

Livia Orlandi has nourished my family with her food and love since before my children were born; I thank her for the dishes from her repertoire that she has allowed me to present as part of my own.

My dear friend Basilio Franchina helped me in so many ways to find the words to share not only recipes but the memories that bring back people and places as well as tastes and aromas.

Learn the rules of the kitchen well, by doing. For the true cook is born when, having assimilated the rules, he or she begins to improvise, to move among the ingredients with a sense of freedom and imagination. Don't be a slave to recipes, to weights and measures, but let your convictions, and above all, love, guide you. In other words, you must be convinced that cooking is an act of love, a gift, a way of sharing with others the little secrets— piccoli segreti *—that are simmering on the burners.*

Italians have never really developed a taste for the prolonged cocktail hour. However, antipasto—literally, "before the meal"—is a course that still traditionally precedes the pasta. Antipasto is almost always served at the table, not while guests are standing about. The dishes are many and varied: vegetables, cooked or not; salumi like prosciutto or salami; crostini; even small slices of frittata. Often, little samples of several of these are served together, and the assortments can vary dramatically from region to region.

In a more contemporary fashion, some antipasti dishes like salads and frittatas are often just right for light meals, suppers, lunches, or brunches. Conversely, you may find side dishes in the vegetable chapter that will do just as nicely as antipasti. This flexibility is at the heart of Italian cuisine.

Antipasti
and Small Dishes

Like all hopeful young actors, I went to a
photographer to get my head shots.
This was soon after Mamma and I moved
to Rome and I was almost 16 years old.

Polenta Crostini

TOASTED POLENTA

Once it cools, polenta becomes firm enough to use as a kind of canapé topped by a variety of ingredients—almost anything you would put on a cracker or bread crostini can be used. Polenta crostini also can be toasted over a charcoal fire, and served as part of a platter of grilled vegetables.

1 recipe Polenta (page 93), poured to a thickness
    of ½ inch and cooled

Soft unsalted butter

To garnish: anchovy fillets, pitted olives, freshly
    grated cheese, chopped tomatoes, thick
    tomato sauce, Ragù alla Napoletana (page 57),
    or pesto

Preheat the broiler.

When the polenta is completely cool and firm, cut it into 1-by-2-inch pieces. Place the pieces on a baking sheet and put it under the broiler for 3 to 5 minutes, until the polenta is crisp and a rich golden color. Do not let the pieces brown.

Spread the butter on the crostini while they are still warm, top them with any of the garnishes, and serve.

Mozzarella in Carrozza

*T*he name of this dish has always seemed a little odd to me, since carrozza *in Italian means carriage or cab. Perhaps the mozzarella is carried along in its little carriage of bread. What is sure is that this is a wonderful and beloved dish, especially popular in the* trattorie *of Rome.*

FOR 6 SERVINGS

1 large (1 pound at least) mozzarella,
   freshly made if possible
12 (½-inch-thick) slices country-style or
   sturdy white bread
½ cup all-purpose flour
4 eggs
Salt
Freshly ground pepper
Olive oil for frying

Remove the crusts from the bread and cut the mozzarella into 6 thick slices. Place each piece of mozzarella between two slices of bread.

Combine the flour with enough warm water to make a thin batter. Dip the mozzarella sandwiches into the batter, coating them lightly on all sides, and place them in a baking dish.

Beat the eggs together with a little salt and pepper and pour the mixture over the sandwiches and into the dish; make sure that enough gets under the sandwiches so that they absorb the egg mixture on both sides, or turn them over. Let the sandwiches soak for about 20 minutes to absorb the egg mixture completely.

Heat at least 1 inch of oil in a large heavy skillet (to about 350° F.). Using a metal spatula, carefully slide the sandwiches into the hot oil. When they are golden on one side, turn them over and fry until the second side is browned, 3 to 5 minutes on each side. Remove them from the pan and set them on paper towels to drain. Serve while still hot.

Fichi al Prosciutto

PROSCIUTTO WITH FIGS

This is a pleasing dish that combines the saltiness of prosciutto with the intensely sweet flesh of figs, but it can only be prepared when figs are in season: usually early summer and September to October, depending on the locale.

FOR 4 TO 5 SERVINGS

1½ tablespoons unsalted butter

3 to 4 tablespoons honey (acacia honey if available)

1 tablespoon white wine vinegar

2 tablespoons muscat wine

12 to 14 very ripe purple or green figs

12 to 14 slices prosciutto

Preheat the oven to 350° F. Place the butter in a small pan or flame-proof dish and melt it over medium heat. Add the honey, vinegar, and wine, bring the mixture to a boil, and boil for 1 minute. Slice the figs into quarters and arrange the pieces on an oven-proof serving platter. Pour the honey mixture over the figs and place the platter in the oven for about 5 minutes. Remove the platter from the oven and set it aside to cool to room temperature. Cut each slice of prosciutto in half lengthwise and crosswise. Wrap a strip around each fig section, return the bundles to the platter, and serve.

EASY ANTIPASTI

Simple, delicious dishes to begin a meal can be made with practically no effort. Light, fresh, and seasonal, their preparations hardly require recipes. Here are a few that are so popular they are well known around the world. As always, use the best ingredients you can find.

Melone e Prosciutto
PROSCIUTTO WITH MELON

Today you can find genuine *prosciutto di Parma* at good specialty food markets and Italian grocers. It's worth the extra cost, but even a good domestic prosciutto can be used. For 6 servings, cut a perfectly ripe, well-chilled honeydew melon into thin, equal slices; peel the slices or not, as you please. Arrange the melon on a platter or individual plates; drape or fold 12 to 18 lean slices of prosciutto over, or wrap the prosciutto around the melon. The melon slices can be placed on a bed of crushed ice if they are to be left out on a buffet table for some time. Of course, you can use other types of melon such as cantaloupe or Galia—but you will need more than one as these are smaller than honeydew.

CLOCKWISE FROM LEFT: Mozzarella in Carrozza, Polenta Crostini, Melone e Prosciutto.

Mozzarella e Pomodori
MOZZARELLA AND TOMATOES

In the summer, you can find this on menus all over Italy, often as *insalata caprese.* Like most simple dishes, *Mozzarella e Pomodori* depends on first-rate ingredients; make it only when locally grown tomatoes are available, and use freshly made mozzarella and extra-virgin olive oil. Thinly slice ripe but firm tomatoes. Overlap the tomatoes with thin slices of fresh mozzarella, top them with fresh basil leaves, and drizzle with olive oil. Black olives, pitted and flattened, or a sprinkle of capers also can be included, or substituted for the basil. With some good bread, this also makes a perfect light lunch.

Bruschetta
GRILLED COUNTRY BREAD

This is truly rustic fare that can be found in country *trattorie*, especially in Lazio, the region around Rome, where a meal hasn't begun until a platter of bruschetta is served. Take several ½- to ⅓-inch-thick slices of bread, preferably from dense, country-style loaves, and toast them on a grill or in a toaster. If necessary, scrape off any burnt bits. Cut a garlic clove in half and rub it over one side of each slice, brush with extra-virgin olive oil, and season as you like with coarse salt and freshly ground pepper. For a dressier version, spread each slice with olive or caper paste. For those who aren't fans of garlic, bruschetta can do without it, but it would be a shame!

Fagioli al Caviale

WHITE BEANS WITH CAVIAR

I've been to Russia several times and once to the Ukraine to make the film Sunflower *with Marcello Mastroianni and the director Vittorio De Sica. In the summer of '97, I was in Moscow, nervously attending a concert conducted by my son Carlo. So I've been fortunate to have had frequent encounters with caviar. Now that fine Iranian caviar is again on the market it is not necessary to travel far to enjoy this treat. At first glance, the pairing of caviar with beans might seem sinful. But remember the Cinderella story, and the splendid prince who falls in love with the humble, poor-as-a-church-mouse Cinderella. Well, marrying beans with caviar has the same charm.*

It is impossible to give quantities for this dish. You must decide according to the number of people you expect, or how much caviar you will purchase. This is an unforgettable flavor, I assure you, with but one drawback—it can be very expensive. Any type of caviar will do—I prefer grey beluga but sevruga and oestra also are fine.

Use white cannellini, Great Northern, or pea beans. Soak them in cold water overnight (or bring the water to a boil, turn off the heat, and let the beans soak for 1 hour); drain them; and cook in fresh water until they are soft but still hold their shape. Drain the beans well. The beans can be served as they are, placed on individual plates and topped with caviar. Or, mash the beans into a paste, spread it over pieces of toasted country-style bread, and then spread a layer of caviar over the beans.

Scenes from Sunflower *with Marcello Mastroianni.*

Fried Neapolitan Pizzas

This is a dish to prepare for the family or a small group of friends with whom you can be very casual, as the pizzas are served almost without interruption as they are cooked, and each person finishes his own and eats it out of hand while it is still warm enough to melt the cheese and bind the flavors.

FOR 4 SERVINGS

2 pounds ripe tomatoes

4 tablespoons olive oil

5 cloves garlic, 2 crushed and 3 minced

¾ pound fresh mozzarella, chopped

½ cup freshly grated Parmigiano cheese

12 basil leaves, chopped

Olive oil for frying

1 recipe Pizza Dough (page 12)

Trim the tomatoes at the stem end, cut them in half, and squeeze out the seeds; chop the tomatoes by hand or in a food processor. Warm the oil in a medium-sized heavy skillet over low heat. Add the crushed garlic and cook until it is lightly browned; add the tomatoes and cook over high heat for about 15 minutes, until the sauce is thick.

Arrange the sauce, cheeses, minced garlic, and basil in small bowls and line a platter or tray with paper towels.

Pour about 1 inch of olive oil into a large heavy skillet and heat it over medium-high heat (to about 350° F.). Using your hands, shape balls of dough about 2 inches in diameter into round flat disks, like miniature pizzas. Fry the disks, 3 or 4 at a time, in the hot oil, turning them until they are golden on both sides. Place the disks on the paper-lined platter to drain very briefly, then let each person help himself, dressing the pizzas with the sauce and other toppings. The pizzas should be folded in half and eaten immediately.

Pizza Rustica

COUNTRY-STYLE PIZZA

This thick pizza is really an egg- and cheese-enriched bread. Serve it sliced, topped with the tomato sauce of your choice or with a selection of salami, olives, hard-boiled eggs, and cheeses. You can start with good-quality store-bought bread dough, or prepare your own dough for simple white bread.

FOR 6 SERVINGS

1½ to 2 pounds bread dough, risen

1½ cups all-purpose flour

4 whole eggs

2 egg yolks

Salt

8 tablespoons olive oil

¼ pound (1 cup) freshly grated Parmigiano cheese

¼ pound (1 cup) shaved pecorino cheese

Freshly ground pepper

Punch down the dough and put it on a board. Knead the dough and flour to combine them well, then form a well in the center. Place the whole eggs and egg yolks, a pinch of salt, and about 1 tablespoon oil into the well. Knead the dough, gradually incorporating the remaining oil and the cheeses, until you have a soft, smooth, and elastic dough. Alternatively, the ingredients can be combined in a food processor and the dough briefly kneaded by hand. Cover the dough with a clean towel and set it in a draft-free spot to rise for 2 hours.

Punch down the dough again, and divide it into two balls. Oil 2 (9- or 10-inch) cake pans and place a ball of dough in each, pressing it with your fingers to cover the bottoms. Cover and let the dough rise in a warm place for 1 hour. Preheat the oven to 400° F. Bake until cooked and golden brown, about 30 minutes.

*Pizzaioli and the huge wood-burning oven at Da Michele,
one of the oldest pizzerias in Naples, where the traditions
of pizza-making are seriously observed.*

Torta di Asparagi

SAVORY ASPARAGUS PIE

FOR 8 ANTIPASTO OR 4 LUNCH OR SUPPER SERVINGS

Tender tops from 2 pounds
    asparagus

8 (½-inch-thick) slices
    country-style or sturdy
    white bread

¾ pound cooked ham

Olive oil

¾ pound soft cheese,
    preferably Italian
    fontina, diced

Preheat the oven to 375° F.

Steam or boil the asparagus for 2 to 3 minutes, until just *al dente* (take care not to overcook them), and refresh them under cold water. Place the asparagus on towels to drain.

Toast the bread. Mince the boiled ham almost to a paste and spread it on the bread. Lightly oil a baking dish large enough to hold the bread slices in one layer; arrange the bread in the dish; then place the asparagus, one beside the other, over the ham. Top with the cheese and bake for 10 to 12 minutes, until the cheese is bubbly and lightly browned. Serve immediately.

Omelet Napoletana

Neapolitan Omelet

6 ounces spaghetti

4 tablespoons unsalted butter

8 eggs

3 tablespoons olive oil

1 tablespoon milk

Pinch of freshly grated nutmeg

Salt

Freshly ground pepper

1 thick slice cooked ham, diced

2 ounces soft cheese such as mozzarella or Italian
  fontina, diced

Freshly grated Parmigiano cheese

1 cup fresh tomato sauce such as *Salsa al Pomodoro
  Semplice* (page 61; optional)

Preheat the oven to 425° F.

Cook the pasta in a generous amount of boiling salted water until just *al dente*; drain well, return the pasta to the pot, and toss with 2 tablespoons butter.

Beat the eggs together with the oil, milk, nutmeg, and salt and pepper to taste. Stir in the ham and soft cheese. Melt the remaining butter in an omelet pan over medium heat and pour in the egg mixture. Lower the heat and cook slowly to set the omelet, taking care to keep the omelet from burning or overcooking on the bottom. Lift the edges with a spatula occasionally to let the uncooked egg run under.

When it is nearly cooked through, slide the omelet onto an oven-proof dish. Place the spaghetti over the omelet and sprinkle with the Parmigiano; place the omelet in the oven for a few minutes, until it is lightly browned on top. Serve hot with the optional tomato sauce.

LE FRITTATE

For home cooks who regard cooking as an enterprise in which thriftiness and resourcefulness are critical, frittatas play an important role. There are almost no leftovers that can't be transformed, with the help of eggs, into flavorful dishes. A frittata is the Italian version of an omelet, and the one here is a good example, but it only hints at the possibilities. Pasta, risotto, polenta, vegetables, meat, and fish all can find a second life as part of a frittata, turning leftovers into a new dish that has its own appeal. Cheese is almost always a good addition, along with any herbs that seem compatible. Of course, you don't need the excuse of leftovers to make a frittata; like other omelets, they have their own reasons for being. Artichokes, mushrooms, zucchini or zucchini flowers, spinach, potatoes, and onions are among the most popular ingredients for frittatas. Like so many other Italian dishes, they can appear in various parts of the menu—for lunch or light dinners, or, in smaller portions, as antipasti or part of a selection of antipasti. And they are convenient because they are even better warm or at room temperature than they are hot out of the pan.

To make a frittata, put some olive oil and a little butter into a skillet—nonstick if possible—and then add whatever leftovers you are using. Depending on the number of people you are serving and the quantity of other ingredients, beat some eggs and season with salt and pepper. Add the eggs to the pan, and cook them over medium heat until a golden crust has formed on the underside. The next part, turning the frittata, is the only real challenge to its preparation, but it can be mastered in a couple of attempts. The traditional method is to cover the skillet with a large platter, and then flip the pan over so that the frittata lands, bottom side up, on the plate; now you slide the frittata, raw side down, back into the skillet. Cook until the second side is also golden brown and the frittata is cooked through.

Alternatively, once the underside is browned, you can slip the skillet into a preheated oven to brown on top and cook through.

La Panzanella

I *don't think you can find a poorer dish than this one. In leaner days it was a very tasty recourse for families who could not put more elaborate or costly dishes on the table; in fact, they could not even afford to waste stale bread. As a child during the war, when I'd see my grandmother busy preparing panzanella, I'd know right away that our household had run out of money. But I loved this kind of food so much that, in absolute childhood innocence, I'd wish those hard times would come upon us more often. Today* panzanella *is enjoyed for its own sake, and because it fits into modern concepts of a healthful diet. It can even be found on the menus of fine restaurants, often at very fancy prices—Nonna Luisa would smile at that.*

FOR 8 ANTIPASTO OR 4 LUNCH OR SUPPER SERVINGS

1½ pounds stale country-style or sturdy white bread,
    sliced 1½ inches thick

6 tablespoons olive oil

Salt

Freshly ground pepper

5 to 6 large ripe tomatoes, chopped

1 medium onion, minced

Small, tender basil leaves

Fresh herbs such as mint and oregano (optional)

Place the bread slices in a shallow dish or pan and add water to cover; set aside to soften for about 20 minutes. Place the slices side by side in a large shallow bowl. Drizzle the oil over the bread, then sprinkle with salt and pepper. Top each slice with the tomatoes, onion, and basil; if necessary, make additional layers to use up all the bread. Let this sit for 20 to 30 minutes, then garnish with more whole basil leaves, and serve. If you wish, you can sprinkle the additional herbs over the *panzanella.*

Two summer salads,
La Panzanella,
and, on the right,
Insalata Ricca.

Soon after we moved to Rome, my mother and I were fortunate to get work as extras in the spectacular American film Quo Vadis. Such opportunities were not frequent enough to provide a steady income, however, and I also worked as a character in Sogno, one of the "fumetti" magazines that were very popular. Fumetti were soap opera stories told in panels of photographs with dialogue coming out of the actors' mouths in little puffs. My name at this time was Sophia Lazzaro.

Insalata Ricca

A Luxurious Salad

FOR **4** TO **6** SERVINGS

5 medium potatoes, cooked

2 red or yellow bell peppers

4 ripe medium tomatoes

10 scallions

2 cups olives, black or green or mixed

4 hard-boiled eggs

¾ pound cooked green beans

12 ounces tuna in oil, drained

6 cornichons, roughly chopped

⅓ cup olive oil

1 teaspoon prepared Dijon-style mustard

2 to 3 tablespoons red wine vinegar

Salt

Freshly ground pepper

Minced herbs such as parsley, thyme, oregano, and basil

4 ounces anchovy fillets, or to taste (optional)

4 walnuts, shelled and coarsely chopped (optional)

This photo is special because it is the first sign of interest the media showed in me. The photographer is an unknown paparazzo. Though I look more like a school girl than a celebrity, I was already known from my apperances in "fumetti." It would be a few years more before anyone recognized me as a film star.

Peel the potatoes, slice them, and place them in a large salad bowl. Remove the stems, ribs, and seeds from the peppers and cut them into strips. Slice the tomatoes. Trim the scallions of their outer skins and all but about 2 inches of their green tops; cut into ½-inch slices. Pit the olives. Cut the eggs lengthwise, then in half horizontally. Cut the green beans into 1-inch pieces.

Flake the tuna over the potatoes; add the tomatoes, peppers, green beans, cornichons, scallions, and olives. Toss gently and garnish with the eggs. In a small bowl beat together the olive oil, mustard, and vinegar to make a smooth vinaigrette; season with salt, pepper, and herbs. Pour the dressing over the salad and garnish with the anchovies and walnuts.

The soups in this collection are of the minestre *type—substantial, rather dense combinations that typically involve pasta, beans, or rice, with greens and other vegetables; meat is included in very small amounts, just to provide flavor. These soups can be served as the main course, and are completely satisfying with bread and salad and perhaps a bit of cheese. I've often wondered why we Italians are partial to* minestre *and I've found the answer in my own taste: We're accustomed to pasta, and we like something chewy between our teeth.*

Soup

Uncle Mario and Aunt Dora Villani at their home in Pozzuoli.
She is another expert cook in the family.

Zuppa di Lenticchie
LENTIL SOUP

Lentils are very commonly used in Italian kitchens, for they are highly nutritious. The best-known lentils in Italy are small and evenly shaped and take their name from Castelluccio, the small rural area in the South where they are grown. Lentils from Castelluccio are worth looking for.

FOR 4 TO 6 SERVINGS

1 pound dried lentils

1 onion, chopped

2 carrots, scraped and chopped

1 branch celery, chopped

Salt

¼ cup extra-virgin olive oil

1 whole clove garlic, peeled

1 ounce anchovy fillets in oil, drained and diced

4 to 6 tomatoes, peeled and chopped

Freshly ground pepper

Italian parsley, minced

Extra-virgin olive oil

A few slices country-style bread, toasted

Cook the lentils, onion, carrots, and celery in salted water for 4 to 5 minutes.

Meanwhile, in a separate large pot, warm ¼ cup oil over low heat and add the garlic. When the garlic begins to turn golden, remove it from the oil and discard. Add the anchovies, tomatoes, and salt and pepper to taste.

Drain the lentils well, reserving the cooking water. Pour them into the saucepan with the tomato mixture, and gradually add cooking water to make a thick soup; cook over medium heat until the lentils are al dente, about 30 minutes. Sprinkle the parsley over and drizzle with extra-virgin olive oil. Serve with the toasted bread on the side.

Il Minestrone

This is the ultimate soup, as it combines many vegetables to create a hearty and nutritious complete meal. Minestrone can even be eaten cool, in the summer. Don't expect to find the same minestrone in different regions of Italy; each place has its preferred recipe, which also changes according to the seasons. Here is a standard version; you can make your own adjustments according to the season and what you find in the market.

For 4 to 5 Servings

2 to 3 tablespoons olive oil

¼ pound pancetta or bacon, chopped

1 large onion, sliced

3 carrots, scraped and thinly sliced

3 to 4 potatoes, peeled and cubed

3 thin zucchini, washed and sliced

1 bunch fresh spinach, washed, trimmed, and
    roughly chopped

1 to 2 stalks celery, trimmed and thinly sliced

½ head cauliflower, separated into flowerets

Salt

Freshly ground pepper

1 cup cooked or canned cannellini or Great Northern
    beans (optional)

2 tomatoes, chopped

Extra-virgin olive oil (optional)

Place 2 to 3 tablespoons oil, the pancetta, and onion in a pot over medium heat. When the onion is golden and the bacon softened, add the carrots, potatoes, zucchini, spinach, celery, and cauliflower. Sauté for about 10 minutes, stirring often, until the vegetables become very lightly browned.

Add enough water to cover the vegetables, bring just to a simmer, and cook over low heat for 20 minutes, or until the vegetables are tender. Add salt to taste; add water if the soup is too thick. Season to taste with pepper, add the tomatoes and beans, and cook until they are heated through.

Adjust the seasoning as necessary, ladle the soup into a tureen or deep serving dish, and serve. At the table, drizzle a thin ribbon of extra-virgin olive oil over each portion if you like.

Fagioli con le Cotiche

BEANS WITH PORK RIND

The summer of 1997 was an unhappy one for me, because I lost my dearest friend and colleague, Marcello Mastroianni. His passing has left a great vacuum in my life. Every once in a while I think of him with emotion and I relive the times when we worked together, our many confidences, our deep, deep friendship. Most characteristic about Marcello was that he had a kind of ironic good will, combined with frankness. Why do I bring him up and talk of the cinema when I should be talking of the kitchen? Because I want to remember his most real and everyday side and because I remember his joyous passion for one dish, which for him excelled those on the most refined menus in the world: Fagioli con le Cotiche, *beans flavored with a pork rind. This is a dish for peasants, for the poor, a dish to be found in the most humble eateries. Perhaps that is why Marcello, a simple man, a friend of common people, favored it. With that thought, and with happiness rather than grief, I offer this robust and satisfying dish.*

Depending on where you live, you may need to order your cotiche *in advance from a butcher or a traditional Italian specialty store. Hispanic markets also often carry* cotiche; *in the South it may be found in stores that specialize in ingredients for regional cooking.*

(continued)

OPPOSITE: Marriage Italian Style;
Marcello and I made twelve films together—this is by far the most famous. RIGHT: A Special Day.

1 pound *cotiche*

Salt

1 pound dried cannellini or Great Northern beans,
    soaked overnight and drained

1 cooked meaty ham bone

1 sprig fresh rosemary

1 tablespoon minced ham fat from the bone

1 clove garlic, crushed

½ onion, chopped

2 tablespoons minced fresh basil

2 tablespoons minced Italian parsley

2 pounds canned peeled tomatoes

Freshly ground pepper

If necessary, quickly pass the *cotiche* over a flame to singe off any bristle. Bring a large pot of water to a boil. Add the *cotiche*, and when the water returns to a boil, lower the heat and simmer for 2 minutes. Drain the *cotiche* in a colander and refresh under cold water; drain well and place on a cutting surface. Refill the pot with water and bring it to a boil. Cut the *cotiche* into 1-inch-square pieces; add the *cotiche* and a pinch of salt to the boiling water, lower the heat, and simmer for 1 to 1½ hours.

Meanwhile, drain the beans and place them with the ham bone and rosemary in a large pot; cover generously with water. Bring to a boil, then lower the heat and simmer until the beans are tender. Drain the *cotiche* and refresh under cold water. Drain the cooked beans and reserve any meat that has fallen off the ham bone.

Place the ham fat, garlic, onion, basil, and parsley in a deep pot or flame-proof casserole over medium-high heat. Sauté briefly, then add the tomatoes, and salt and pepper to taste; bring to a boil, then lower the heat and simmer for about 20 minutes. Add the *cotiche*, beans, and ham, continue to cook for 10 minutes, then serve.

Minestra di Riso, Patate, e Fagioli

RICE, POTATO, AND BEAN SOUP

FOR 6 SERVINGS

½ pound dried cannellini or Great Northern beans,
  soaked overnight

1 pound potatoes, peeled and cubed

1 onion, chopped

1 small stalk celery, chopped

¼ pound pancetta or slab bacon, diced

2 fresh or 1 dried bay leaf

1 ½ quarts or more good-quality vegetable broth

1 cup uncooked white rice

Salt

Freshly ground pepper

Extra-virgin olive oil

Freshly grated Parmigiano cheese

Drain the beans and place them with the potatoes, onion, celery, pancetta, and bay leaves in a large pot. Cover with the broth, bring to a boil, then lower the heat and simmer for about 30 minutes, until the beans and potatoes are tender but not mushy. Add additional broth or water if the soup becomes too thick.

Meanwhile, cook the rice. When the soup is ready, add the rice and cook just to heat through. Season to taste with salt and pepper; remove and discard the bay leaves. At the table, pour a thin ribbon of extra-virgin olive oil and sprinkle grated cheese over each serving.

Pasta e Fagioli

It is hard to imagine another dish that is so typical of the Italian table; in virtually every region, province, and even in some small villages you can find a unique version of pasta and beans in combination. The types of pasta and beans themselves change from place to place, along with the ingredients that make up the broth and give it its flavor. There are versions that contain a lot of meat, many—like this one—that are flavored with just a bit of meat, and others that are completely vegetarian.

FOR 6 TO 8 SERVINGS

½ large onion, peeled

1 celery heart, washed

6 fresh large basil leaves

1 clove garlic, peeled

¼ pound pancetta or bacon

1 tablespoon olive oil

1 tablespoon unsalted butter

2 pounds cooked (1 pound raw) borlotti, cannellini, or Great Northern beans; cooking water reserved

¾ pound dried pasta such as linguine, fettuccine, or papardelle, roughly broken by hand

Chop the onion, celery, basil, garlic, and pancetta. Heat the oil and butter in a deep pot or casserole; add the chopped ingredients and cook over medium-high heat, stirring, for 2 minutes. Add the beans and their cooking water.

When the vegetables are soft, add enough hot water to cover generously. When the liquid comes to a boil, add the pasta and cook until just *al dente*; serve at once.

VARIATIONS: To make a thick soup, the beans can be puréed before the pasta is added, in which case additional water probably will be needed to keep the pasta from sticking as it cooks. Or, just a cup or so of the beans can be removed, puréed, and then stirred back into the soup before the pasta is added.

Minestra di Fave

FAVA BEAN SOUP

This is a dish you can prepare only in the springtime, when fava beans are in season. Dried favas don't have the same special and unmistakable flavor as fresh favas, but you can use dried favas in the soup with good results. If you do use dried fava beans, adjust the quantity to 1 pound, soak them in water at least overnight, and then skin them before using. The addition of canned tuna may seem unusual, but when I was growing up it was quite cheap, and often used as a way of flavoring otherwise meager dishes.

FOR 6 SERVINGS

2¼ pounds fresh fava beans in their pods, or
   1 pound if already shelled

3 tablespoons olive oil

2 ounces bacon, diced

1 large onion, diced

3 to 3½ ounces tuna (brands vary), imported Italian
   if possible, drained and flaked

Salt

Freshly ground pepper

2 tablespoons minced Italian parsley

Croutons made from toasted bread (optional)

Remove the fava beans from their pods. If they are small, they will need no further preparation. If they are large, and the skin that surrounds each bean seems tough, remove the skin with a paring knife. This can be facilitated by dropping the beans into a pot of boiling water for a few seconds and then refreshing them quickly under cold water; the beans can then be easily slipped out of their skins.

Warm the oil in a soup pot, add the bacon, onion, and tuna, and sauté over low heat. When the onion begins to turn golden, add the fava beans, let them absorb the juices for a minute or two, then add water to cover the ingredients by ¼ inch. Add salt and pepper to taste, and cook at a low simmer until the beans are just tender. Stir in the parsley and cook for 2 to 3 minutes longer. Place a small handful of croutons into each soup plate and ladle the soup over.

Pasta, as we know, is the ultimate Italian creation. There are those who have rummaged through history and attempted to trace the origins of pasta to noodles made hundreds, perhaps thousands, of years ago in China. The myth is that Marco Polo returned from his travels and introduced the noodle into Italian culture. It may be true that the Chinese also came up with this concept, but it can be documented that pasta existed in the West—Italy, specifically—in ancient Roman times. Pasta, in short, was born in Italy, more precisely in the south. Today it reigns on tables, in every part of the globe, especially in its most classic form: with various kinds of tomato sauce.

Pasta

Like the end of a fairy tale, the little girl from Pozzuoli who watched movies like Blood and Sand *countless times has arrived in Hollywood. The year was 1956. Almost from the beginning, interviewers have asked me what diet I follow to stay in shape. It amuses me to see their expressions when I answer, "Pasta." It is only a slight exaggeration; I adore pasta and eat it almost every day. And it is a healthful food, especially when served with tomatoes or other vegetable-based sauces.*

Pasta Basics

A plate of pasta, sublime as it may be, is far more complex than it may appear. Like most simple dishes, the quality of the ingredients and care in their preparation are critical to success. Nevertheless, the rules, once learned, are few and easy to follow.

BUYING PASTA

Pasta must be made with flour milled from hard wheat. Make sure that the product you buy, whether imported or domestic, meets this requisite. Pasta made from other types of wheat will become mushy, doughy, and limp when cooked or it may cook unevenly, remaining hard at the center when the exterior is well cooked.

COOKING GUIDELINES

❑ Cook pasta in a generous amount of water—4 quarts for each pound is a good ratio, but if your pot is large enough, use even more, but not so much that it will overflow when you put in the pasta. Add a large pinch of salt to the water when it comes to a boil, not sooner. And remember that while salt is essential, too much is as bad as too little.

❑ Pasta must be eaten *al dente* or it will be limp and tasteless. *Al dente* means that the pasta must give some resistence to the the teeth, so, after buying first-quality pasta, the second most important rule is to be attentive to the cooking time. The packages of most brands carry recommended cooking times, but let me give you some personal advice: Stop cooking the pasta *1 minute* before the time suggested.

❑ Drain the pasta well in a colander before pouring it into a dry serving bowl.

❑ Once the pasta is in the bowl, pour over just enough sauce to cover, and toss the pasta well. The strands must be evenly coated, but not oversauced. Additional sauce can be offered at the table. Almost indispensible with *pastasciutta*—pasta served in sauce—is freshly grated cheese, though it is usually omitted with fish or shellfish sauces. The cheese of choice is Parmigiano except for certain dishes in which another type, such as pecorino, is integral.

Pasta Shapes

There are shapes to please everyone's eye and palate, some quite fanciful and charming. Pasta shapes have their practical aspects as well, and the recipes in this chapter include suggestions for the types best suited for them. In general, long pastas, such as spaghetti, spaghettini, capelli di angeli (thin "angel hair"), linguine (flattened, "little tongues"), and bucatini (thick, with holes running through the centers), among others, are best with light or thin sauces that coat the strands. Short pasta with large holes or textured surfaces are usually used with thick, chunky sauces like ragù. This group includes macaroni (short, dried pasta), penne (quill-shaped), rigatoni (ridged tubes), fusilli (corkscrews), farfalle (bowties), and conchiglie (shells). In each category there are dozens of other choices, but you should always think of your sauce before you pick your pasta.

Fresh Pasta

Dried pasta (*paste secche*) is the most commonly used and most easily found. But a discussion of pasta would be incomplete if we didn't include *paste fresche*, or freshly made pasta. Fresh pasta has its own special taste and a texture that is at once firm and elastic. A few years ago, when fresh pasta first became widely popular here, some people seemed to think that it was superior to dried. It is important to remember that fresh and dried are simply different but equal, suitable for specific preparations in the same way that different shapes are.

Preparing fresh pasta is a delicate affair that requires some skill, experience, and time. However, many good specialty food shops offer fresh pasta in many forms, from long flat lasagne, fettucine, and tagliatelle, to short shapes like cavatelli and farfalle. You also may find filled varieties like ravioli and tortelloni. If you wish to make your own filling but not the pasta itself, you can buy sheets of pasta ready for this purpose, or you may be able to order some from a shop.

Pasta and its Sauces

Pastasciutta is dried pasta—*asciutta* means dried—but the word also is used in a more general way to refer to pasta topped with sauce, rather than served in soup or broth.

Fresh Pasta Dough

FOR **4** TO **6** SERVINGS

4 cups all-purpose flour
6 large egg yolks
Salt

Make a mound of the flour on a work surface. Make a well in the center of the flour then drop in the egg yolks one at a time, gradually incorporating the flour. Add a pinch of salt. By the time the final egg has been added, all or almost all the flour should have been incorporated.

Flour your hands and knead the dough until a smooth, uniform, and solid mass is formed. Maintain a steady rhythm and be patient; the process may take 15 to 20 minutes, depending on the pressure you exert and numerous other factors, including the weather. Very small amounts of flour can be added if the dough seems too moist; conversely, water can be incorporated by the tablespoon if the dough is too dry to work.

Cover the dough with a clean cloth and allow it to rest for 30 minutes. Place the dough on the floured work surface and knead it again for a few minutes. Divide the dough into two pieces. Using your hands, stretch the dough a bit, then use a rolling pin to roll it out to the appropriate thickness for the pasta you will be making. Use a sharp knife or ravioli cutter to cut the sheets into the shapes required by your recipe.

If you have one, a manual (not electric) pasta machine can be used. Once the dough has been formed it can be kneaded by passing it through the widest setting 10 or 12 times. Then, beginning again with the widest, continue to pass the dough through, narrowing the setting each time. Finally, cut the pasta into the desired shape on the machine or by hand.

Timpano di Carne e Pomodoro

BAKED PASTA WITH MEAT AND TOMATOES

The advantage of this way of preparing pasta is that it is assembled in advance and shaped like a shallow cake that can then be cooked to serve or even transported beyond the table—to a picnic or to present as a culinary gift. You can make the fresh tagliatelle or buy it at a store that sells fresh pasta; if tagliatelle is not available, fettucine can be substituted.

FOR 6 SERVINGS

4 tablespoons olive oil

6 tablespoons unsalted butter

¾ pound ground meat, beef and pork combined

½ cup white wine

Salt

Freshly ground pepper

1½ pounds fresh tagliatelle (page 51)

2½ cups simple homemade tomato sauce such as
    Salsa al Pomodoro Semplice (page 61) or good-
    quality store-bought

½ cup freshly grated Parmigiano cheese

Fresh basil leaves

4 egg yolks

1 tablespoon all-purpose flour

½ cup heavy cream

Olive oil

Fine, dry bread crumbs

Heat the oil and butter in a saucepan over medium heat until the butter is melted; add the meat and brown it thoroughly, breaking it up with a wooden fork or spoon. Pour in the wine and cook over medium heat until it evaporates; add salt and pepper to taste.

Meanwhile, bring a large pot of water to a boil, add a pinch of salt, and drop in the tagliatelle. Cook the pasta until just *al dente*; take care not to overcook the pasta, as it will cook a bit more when baked. Drain the pasta and refresh it under cold water.

Preheat the oven to 350° F.

Place the tagliatelle in a large mixing bowl and toss it with the tomato sauce, ¼ cup cheese, and the basil. In the top of a double boiler beat the egg yolks with the flour, the remaining cheese, the cream, and salt and pepper to taste. Place the top over simmering water in the bottom of the double boiler and cook, stirring, to reduce and thicken the sauce; take care not to let the eggs curdle. Add the egg mixture to the tagliatelle and combine well.

Oil the bottom and sides of a deep—round, if possible—oven-proof dish and coat it with bread crumbs. Arrange the tagliatelle in the dish and top with a light layer of bread crumbs. Bake, uncovered, for 1 hour, or until browned and slightly crisp on top. Serve the *timpano* from the baking dish.

FOLLOWING PAGES: *Modern Naple with the ancient Vesuvius still looming over her.*

Ragù alla Napoletana

NEAPOLITAN STUFFED BEEF ROLLS AND SAUCE

For me, born in the shadow of Mount Vesuvius, Ragù alla Napoletana *is the epitome of pasta sauces. The word* ragù *comes from the French* ragout, *a linguistic gift from the time that Naples was ruled by the Bourbons; together Sicily and Naples were known as the Kingdom of the Two Sicilies. The taking of Sicily, and then Naples, by Garibaldi was the turning point in the movement to unify Italy. Today the phonetic version of the word* ragù *is used throughout the country for rich, meaty sauces, like Ragù Bolognese, which is almost as famous as the ragù of Naples.*

A Neapolitan ragù is made with involtini—*thin slices of meat, generally beef or veal, rolled around a simple, flavorful stuffing and gently braised. Traditionally, the resulting sauce is served over pasta and the meat follows as the second course with a vegetable or salad. This is the classic meal for Sunday family dinners.*

FOR 6 SERVINGS

6 slices beef, each weighing ⅓ pound

Generous handful of minced Italian parsley

6 slices bacon

2 cloves garlic, chopped

3 to 4 tablespoons extra-virgin olive oil

1 cup white wine

5 to 6 pounds peeled tomatoes, chopped

Salt

Freshly ground pepper

1¼ pounds penne, rigatoni,
  or bucatini

(continued)

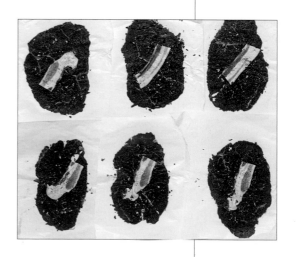

Pat the meat slices dry and, with a meat pounder or the side of a large chef's knife or cleaver, pound them to a thickness of about ¼ inch. Sprinkle the parsley over the slices. Place a slice of bacon on each piece of meat, divide the garlic among them, and season with salt and pepper. Starting from the narrowest end, roll up each slice and secure it closed with a toothpick.

Heat the oil over medium heat in a pan just large enough to hold the rolls in one layer. Place the rolls in the oil and brown them gently on all sides. As they brown, moisten the rolls with small amounts of the wine. When the wine is used up and the rolls are golden brown, add the tomatoes, lower the heat, cover the pan, and let the ragù simmer slowly for 2 hours, or until the meat is fork tender. Turn the rolls from time to time. Adjust the seasoning, adding salt and pepper to taste. The sauce is ready to use. It can be made several days in advance.

Cook the pasta until just *al dente*, drain, and ladle the sauce over. Follow with the meat or save it for another meal.

SOPHIA LOREN'S • RECIPES & MEMORIES

THE RITUAL OF RAGÙ

*T*he great Neapolitan actor, Eduardo De Filippo also was one of Italy's premier playwrights. De Filippo was a keen interpreter of the Neapolitan reality—the glory as well as the misery—and left many theatrical landmarks.

It was my good fortune to be able to interpret his masterpiece, *Filumena Marturano, Marriage Italian Style* in the film version. That film remains in my career and in my heart one of the happiest, partly because it brings memories of my dear friends Marcello Mastroianni and Vittorio De Sica.

But that was not my only film based on a work of De Filippo. A few years ago I played in another of his comedies, *Saturday, Sunday and Monday*. This is a work that digs deeply into the Neapolitan soul, with all its virtues, vices, and infinite imaginativeness. The story is set entirely around the weekly ritual of *Ragù alla Napoletana*: preparations on Saturday, serving the dish at Sunday dinner, and the aftermath on Monday. The woman at the center of the story officiates over her kitchen with undisputed authority.

Other themes are woven into the narrative: jealousy, love, the wearing down of feelings, virtuousness, and the effrontery of the dozen or so people who buzz around the celebration of this representative Sunday ragù. In other words, ragù is rooted in a nearly sacred tradition and in the soul and customs of my Naples. Today, when the scent of ragù comes from my kitchen in Geneva or Los Angeles, or from my sister's in Rome, it's as if the bells are ringing out a feast day as they did when, in my childhood, ragù would arrive on our meager table, managed heroically by my grandparents.

Pasta con Crema di Gorgonzola

PASTA WITH GORGONZOLA CREAM

Gorgonzola is a magnificent soft, creamy-textured cheese made from the milk of Alpine cows. One of the world's finest blue-veined cheeses, it is buttery and full of characteristic little greenish lines and cavities. It is similar to French Roquefort, but Roquefort is firmer, less creamy, and doesn't melt as easily as Gorgonzola. In fact, there is more than one type of Gorgonzola, and a small selection is beginning to appear in American markets. If you have the choice, I recommend Gorgonzola dolce for this sauce, but the more familiar piccante also will be fine.

Gorgonzola can be an extraordinary resource when you must improvise a meal in a hurry. In fact, you can prepare this Gorgonzola sauce in just a few minutes, in the time it takes to cook your pasta; this is elegant fast food.

This is a good sauce for rigatoni, but if you wish to use fresh pasta, choose tagliolini; this sauce coats the noodles nicely.

FOR 6 SERVINGS

Generous ½ pound Gorgonzola cheese

2 tablespoons unsalted butter

1 small stalk celery, roughly chopped

½ onion, roughly chopped

Salt

Freshly ground pepper

½ cup heavy cream

1 cup milk

1 hard-boiled egg yolk (optional)

Handful of finely minced Italian parsley

2 cloves garlic, peeled

1½ pounds rigatoni or fresh tagliolini

Place the Gorgonzola, butter, celery, onion, garlic, and a pinch of pepper in a blender or the work bowl of a food processor. Process to a smooth paste; when the mixture is well blended, add the cream, milk, and egg yolk; add the parsley and salt to taste. Blend until the sauce is very smooth. Meanwhile, cook the pasta until just *al dente*, then toss it with the sauce.

Spaghetti con Salsa al Pomodoro Semplice
SPAGHETTI WITH BASIC TOMATO SAUCE

The addition of sugar to the sauce may seem surprising, but it is not at all unusual for good Italian home cooks. The sugar is not to make the sauce sweet, but to balance the acid of the tomatoes. Today in the United States the acid level is not so high in some tomatoes, so you may want to taste the tomatoes first and add the sugar if it is necessary.

FOR 6 SERVINGS

6 tablespoons extra-virgin olive oil

4 to 5 cloves garlic, crushed or chopped

1½ to 2 pounds peeled and crushed ripe tomatoes

Fresh basil leaves

1 teaspoon sugar

Salt

Freshly ground pepper

1½ pounds thin spaghetti

Freshly ground Parmigiano cheese

Place the oil in a saucepan over high heat. Add the garlic and sauté until lightly browned. Remove and discard the garlic; add the tomatoes, basil, sugar, and salt and pepper to taste. Simmer the sauce over low heat for about 30 minutes, stirring occasionally. Meanwhile, cook the pasta until just *al dente*, drain, and toss it with the sauce. Sprinkle with the cheese.

Spaghetti con Pomodoro Crudo
SPAGHETTI WITH UNCOOKED TOMATO SAUCE

Cool and refreshing, this is excellent summer fare, especially with a chilled light white wine. You can top the spaghetti with grated Parmigiano, but it isn't essential.

FOR 6 SERVINGS

1½ pounds spaghetti

2 pounds tomatoes, not quite ripe, chopped

½ pound fresh mozzarella, thinly sliced

2 medium red or Vidalia onions (or less), thinly sliced

¼ cup pitted Sicilian green olives, roughly chopped

2 tablespoons drained capers

¼ cup minced Italian parsley

10 to 12 chopped fresh oregano leaves or
   ¼ teaspoon dried

1 to 2 cloves garlic, crushed

Salt

Freshly ground pepper

⅓ cup extra-virgin olive oil

Freshly grated Parmigiano cheese (optional)

Cook the pasta until just *al dente*. While the pasta is cooking, place in a large serving bowl the tomatoes, mozzarella, onions, olives, capers, parsley, oregano, garlic, and salt and pepper to taste. Pour the oil over and toss gently.

When the pasta is ready, pour it into a colander and quickly rinse it under cold water; drain well and add the warm spaghetti to the bowl. Toss to combine, remove the garlic if desired, and serve. Pass the cheese at the table.

Spaghetti con Burro di Acciuga
SPAGHETTI WITH ANCHOVY BUTTER SAUCE

Do not serve cheese with this dish, which tastes strongly of the sea.

FOR 6 SERVINGS

6 tablespoons unsalted butter

5 anchovy fillets in oil, drained

3 cloves garlic, crushed

2 tablespoons olive oil

¾ pound ripe tomatoes, peeled and crushed

Salt

Freshly ground pepper

2 tablespoons minced Italian parsley

1½ pounds spaghetti

In a stone mortar or large bowl or food processor, mash or process the butter and anchovies to a smooth paste. Shape the mixture into a ball and refrigerate until ready to use. Put the oil and garlic in a pan, heat, and when the garlic has flavored the oil without burning, add the tomatoes and a pinch of salt and pepper. Cook the sauce for 10 to 12 minutes. Remove from the heat and add the parsley.

Meanwhile, cook the spaghetti in a separate pot until just *al dente*. Place the chilled anchovy butter in a serving bowl; add the pasta and toss well and thoroughly so that the anchovy butter softens and coats the strands of spaghetti. Pour in the tomato sauce and toss carefully until the sauce is well incorporated. Serve at once.

Bucatini all' Amatriciani

BUCATINI IN THE AMATRICE STYLE

This is a sauce that comes from Amatrice, a charming little mountain town not far from Rome. It's a hearty sauce, made the way the mountain people prefer their food, especially the hardworking men who descend into the valleys anticipating the robust, intense flavors emanating from their wives' pots and pans. The preferred pasta for this is bucatini—thick spaghetti with holes through the center—but if that is not available, a thick spaghetti will do.

FOR 6 SERVINGS

6 tablespoons olive oil

2 tablespoons unsalted butter

2 ounces pancetta or bacon, diced

3 onions, thinly sliced

½ medium fresh or dried chile pepper, minced or crushed

1 pound fresh or good-quality canned peeled tomatoes, crushed

6 large or 8 medium fresh basil leaves

Salt

Freshly grated pecorino cheese

1¼ pounds bucatini or thick spaghetti

Place the oil and butter in a skillet over medium heat; add the pancetta and onions. When the onions begin to turn golden, add the chile pepper, tomatoes, basil, and a pinch of salt. Cook the sauce for about 15 minutes, until the flavors are nicely combined.

Meanwhile, cook the pasta until just *al dente*; drain. Toss the pasta with the sauce and sprinkle generously with cheese.

Bucatini alla Carbonara

The film Two Women *was shot mostly in a mountainous region two to three hours from Rome. Not so far, but it seems like another universe from the lowlands. Unlike city dwellers, especially Romans, mountain people are used to long silences, and they are simple and direct in their manner. Their cuisine is similar—hearty, substantial, and nourishing.*

Not far from our location was a small all-male community of charcoal workers. This trade must be almost extinct, because no one needs coal any more, and even country stoves now use natural gas or electricity. There is still some demand for charcoal or wood for some types of traditional cooking in fireplaces and for grilling, roasting, and rotisserie-style cooking.

But to return to my mountain people, they offered the cast and crew this pasta dish, Maccheroni alla Carbonara. *The* maccheroni—*the pasta—were homemade, long, rather*

thick strands, with no hole through the center, irreverently called strozzapreti. *("priest stranglers"). Our incomparable director, Vittorio De Sica, and I asked for seconds, and I made sure I was invited the next day to stand beside the men at the fire and take notes on the recipe.*

By now I've prepared and eaten Bucatini alla Carbonara *many times in my life. This recipe is faithful to the way the men prepared it, but it will never have the same flavor as it did then. Whenever I have* La Carbonara *I become nostalgic for those people and places.*

Carbonara *is often served with a healthy sprinkling of freshly ground pepper over it, which some food scholars maintain represents a dusting of carbon powder. There also are those who say the dish was*

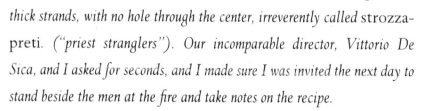

LEFT: *A scene from* Two Women. RIGHT: *My dear friend, the unforgettable maestro Vittorio De Sica, carried my Oscar for* Two Women *from Los Angeles to Rome.*

invented because the essential ingredients, bacon and eggs, were supplied by American GIs to cooks using charcoal burners in Rome itself, but my experience would disprove this. Probably the GIs were simply the source of ingredients for a dish that already existed. In any case, Bucatini alla Carbonara remains a Roman specialty that a number of restaurants proudly prepare. If you cannot find bucatini, use thick spaghetti or penne.

FOR 6 SERVINGS

---

1 tablespoon olive oil

2 tablespoons unsalted butter

4 ounces pancetta or bacon, diced

Generous pinch of minced Italian parsley

5 or 6 egg yolks

2 tablespoons light cream

3 tablespoons freshly grated pecorino or Parmigiano
cheese, plus additional to serve

1¼ pounds bucatini

Heat the oil and butter in a pan, then add the pancetta and parsley; sauté over medium heat to brown the pancetta well. In a bowl beat together the eggs yolks, cream, and cheese.

Meanwhile, cook the bucatini until just *al dente* . Drain the pasta well, and turn it out into a serving dish. Working quickly, pour first the pancetta mixture, then the beaten egg mixture over the pasta. Toss quickly to coat the strands with the sauce; the eggs will cook in the heat of the pasta. Serve immediately while still hot. Pass additional cheese at the table.

OPPOSITE: *Bucatini alla Carbonara*

Linguine con Salsa Sophia
LINGUINE WITH SOPHIA'S SAUCE

I don't presume to compete with the great professional chefs, but in my own little way, and every once in a while, I create a recipe that is enthusiastically received. The one here was inspired by the one for Pesto Genovese, made with some different ingredients, but executed by the traditional method. To me, pounding the ingredients in a mortar is the only way to make pesto (to pound, in Italian, is pestare), but you may prefer to use a blender or food processor. If you do make a pesto by machine, take care not to overblend—the sauce should be smooth, but with some texture. I like this sauce on linguine or spaghetti—but not thin spaghetti. Do not serve cheese with this.

2 cups Italian parsley leaves

3 cloves garlic, peeled

¼ cup pinoli

3 to 4 anchovy fillets in salt, rinsed of excess salt

10 or more black olives, roughly chopped

2 tablespoons capers, drained

1 small onion, minced

About ¼ cup extra-virgin olive oil

1 pound linguine or spaghetti

Freshly ground pepper or paprika

In a mortar, pound together the parsley, garlic, pinoli, anchovies, olives, capers, and onion until the ingredients are uniformly combined. Gradually pour in the oil, continuing to pound the paste, adding the oil very slowly until the paste is thick and saucelike. Set the sauce aside until the pasta is ready.

Cook the pasta until just *al dente*. Place a lightly oiled pan over medium heat. Drain the pasta and toss it into the pan. Cook the pasta for under a minute, until it dries completely and just begins to brown. Place the pasta in a serving bowl and toss with the sauce and a dusting of pepper or paprika.

OPPOSITE: *Ingredients for my salsa and a typical wooden grinder used to reduce them to a paste. Such simple, efficient appliances once were common in Neapolitan kitchens—this one looks handmade and probably dates from the late 1800s.*
RIGHT: *Salsa Sophia.*

Trenette con Pesto Genovese
THIN NOODLES WITH PESTO

Trenette are long, thin, and flat pasta, like narrow ribbons; they are used fresh as well as seccha, or dried. Similar to linguine ("little tongues"), they are the typical pasta for one of Italy's most renowned sauces, the superb pesto of Genoa. Genoa is the principal city of the region of Liguria, where a great variety of herbs grow abundantly. Foremost among them is basil, which is the foundation of this sauce; the other ingredients are good grated cheese, olive oil, and garlic.

To me, a genuine pesto must be made by pounding the ingredients with a mortar and pestle, but if you must use a machine, take care that you produce a textured paste, not a thin liquid.

FOR 4 TO 6 SERVINGS

3 cloves garlic, peeled

3 cups fresh basil leaves, wiped clean

3 tablespoons freshly grated Parmigiano cheese

3 tablespoons freshly grated pecorino cheese

About ½ cup extra-virgin olive oil

Salt

1¼ pounds trenette or linguine

Place the garlic and basil in the mortar, then pound them with the pestle until they are well integrated. Add the cheeses and pound until the ingredients are well incorporated. Gradually add the oil, very slowly, drop by drop, continuing to pound the paste. It is difficult to say just how much oil you will need, but the result should be a sauce that still resembles a paste, but a thick, somewhat runny one. Taste and add salt if necessary.

If you use an electric blender or food processor, follow the sequence above, and use a start-and-stop method, so that you control the texture; if you process the ingredients all at once or too quickly, you will produce a bright green thin liquid, not a characteristic pesto. Cook the pasta until just *al dente*, drain, toss with the sauce, and serve at once.

Tagliatelle con Zucchini
TAGLIATELLE WITH ZUCCHINI

Zucchini sometimes seems to be rather bland, and not very interesting. But at the same time, it has a distinctive taste and great versatility. It is very good in numerous pasta dishes, such as this one. Perhaps we underestimate this simple, ubiquitous vegetable.

FOR 6 SERVINGS

2 pounds young, thin zucchini

Olive oil

¼ cup freshly grated Parmigiano and
   pecorino cheeses, combined

Salt

Freshly ground pepper

1½ pounds fresh tagliatelle or spaghetti

8 to 10 large basil leaves, cut into shreds

Cut the zucchini into ½-inch rounds. Heat ¼ inch of oil in a large heavy skillet over medium-high heat. When the oil is hot, add the zucchini slices and fry until they are golden brown on both sides; add more oil as needed. As they cook, place the zucchini slices on paper towels to drain.

Cook the pasta until just *al dente*, drain, and place in a serving bowl. Add the zucchini, cheeses, salt and pepper to taste, and some of the oil from the pan, and toss well. Sprinkle individual servings with the basil.

Spaghetti al Limone
SPAGHETTI WITH LEMON

FOR 6 SERVINGS

3 tablespoons unsalted butter

2 cloves garlic

Zest of 2 to 3 lemons, minced

½ cup heavy cream

Salt

Freshly ground pepper

1½ pounds spaghetti

Freshly grated Parmigiano cheese (optional)

Melt the butter in a large saucepan or skillet over medium heat. Add the garlic and sauté until golden; add the lemon zest, ¼ cup cream, and salt and pepper to taste. Remove and discard the garlic if you like.

Meanwhile, cook the pasta until just *al dente*. Drain the pasta and add it to the saucepan along with the remaining cream. Toss well for a couple of minutes, remove from the heat, and serve. Pass the cheese at the table.

Penne alla Puttanesca

PASTA QUILLS, WHORE STYLE

Don't be scandalized by the name for this dish, which, in dialect, invokes the world's oldest profession, that of the prostitute. When women order penne alla puttanesca *in restaurants, you may hear comments like "How naughty!" and detect hidden meanings but in fact, the term also indicates vitality and gaiety. Once particularly popular in the towns outside Rome, you can now find this dish all over Italy. I definitely prefer penne as the pasta of choice for* alla puttanesca *but bucatini or spaghetti also can be used. Some interpretations of the name suggest that this dish is fast enough for a "working girl" to prepare between assignations; what is certain is that it is as good as it is fast.*

FOR 4 SERVINGS

Salt

1 pound penne

4 anchovy fillets, drained

2 cloves garlic

2 tablespoons extra-virgin olive oil

3 tablespoons unsalted butter

2 to 3 large tomatoes, peeled, seeded, and chopped

½ cup pitted black olives, finely chopped

1 tablespoon capers, drained

¼ cup minced Italian parsley

Bring a large pot of water to a boil, add a pinch of salt, and drop in the pasta.

In a mortar, pound the anchovies and garlic to a paste with a pestle. (Alternatively, finely chop them.) Heat the oil and butter in a pan, add the paste, and sauté for about 1 to 2 minutes over medium heat. Add the tomatoes, olives, and capers, and cook for 15 minutes.

When the pasta is *al dente*, drain it and dress it with the sauce. Sprinkle with the parsley and serve.

Spaghetti con Vongole
SPAGHETTI WITH CLAMS

This recipe works as well for mussels and shrimp, or a combination.

FOR 6 SERVINGS

2 pounds clams, well scrubbed

4 tablespoons chopped Italian parsley

⅓ cup olive oil

3 cloves garlic, chopped

2 pounds chopped fresh tomatoes or drained canned tomatoes

1¼ pounds spaghetti, vermicelli, or linguine

Place the clams in a deep pot, cover, and place over medium-high heat. After a few minutes, open the pot and remove any clams that have opened. Cover the pot again, and continue to check and remove open clams as soon as you can so that they do not overcook and toughen. Once all the clams are removed, pour their cooking liquid through a sieve and reserve it. Put the clams into a bowl and sprinkle with some of the parsley. (If you prefer, the clams can be removed from their shells.)

Heat the oil in a medium-sized pan, add the garlic, and cook it briefly, just until it begins to color. Add the tomatoes and cook over medium heat for 15 minutes; add the clam liquid, raise the heat, and cook until the sauce thickens, about 10 minutes. Add the clams and cook briefly.

Meanwhile, cook the pasta until just *al dente*, drain it, and turn it out into a serving dish. Pour the sauce over, top with the remaining parsley, and serve at once. Or, if your pan is large enough, you can add the pasta to the sauce just long enough to toss and combine.

Rice dishes, even in their most exotic preparations, rarely take longer to cook than pasta. Their omission would represent a serious gap in a book of Italian cookery. Besides the recipes here, keep in mind that almost all the sauces I've included for pasta work well with rice, from Ragù alla Napoletana *to* Pesto Genovese *to* Salsa Sophia. *All you need to know is how to cook rice.*

Polenta is nearly as versatile and certainly as nutritious.

Rice & Polenta

*While in Capri to make
It Started in Naples,
I was able to visit
my grandfather at his
house in Pozzuoli. I also
saw my Aunt Dora,
my mother's sister, and old
friends and neighbors.*
Opposite: *I worked in the
movie with Clark Gable,
who adored Neapolitan
cooking. In the beginning,
Gable's character is hostile
toward mine, but things
thaw in my kitchen and
lead to love—though he
doesn't seem to appreciate
my efforts in this scene.*

RISOTTO BASICS

Once mastered, making risotto is a pleasant and satisfying process. The steps here can be applied to most recipes, including the ones in this book, unless another method is indicated. In time, you'll probably develop your own combinations of broth, flavorings, and other ingredients, especially vegetables.

❑   Heat the oil, butter, or whatever other fat you're using in a medium-sized heavy pan. Add the flavorings, such as onion, garlic, mushrooms, or herbs called for in your recipe, and sauté briefly; add the rice and cook until it is opaque, about 30 seconds. In some recipes, wine is added at this point and cooked until absorbed and nearly evaporated.

❑   Now the liquid, usually broth, is added very gradually to the rice mixture. Heat the liquid in a pan or in a microwave oven. Keep the rice over medium heat, and, with a ladle, add the broth gradually to the rice—½ to 1 cup at a time. Stir the liquid into the rice and let it simmer, while you continue to stir, until it is almost completely absorbed, then add another ladleful of broth. Continue this process until the rice is cooked, but not mushy—*al dente*, as with pasta—and creamy, but not soupy in texture.

❑   Depending on your recipe, cheese or other seasonings are added and then the rice served at once.

A Note About the Rice

The best rice to use for risotto is imported from Italy and is quite easy to find in Italian markets, specialty food shops, and many supermarkets. Several types are available. You may like to experiment and choose your own favorite.

Risotto con Piselli

RISOTTO WITH PEAS

FOR 6 SERVINGS

---

2 tablespoons olive oil

3 ounces (about 6 strips) bacon, diced

1 medium onion, diced

1 small carrot, scraped and diced

Big pinch chopped Italian parsley

4 or 5 basil leaves, chopped

1 pound crushed fresh or canned tomatoes

2 medium zucchini, thinly sliced

1 pound fresh pea pods, to yield about 1 cup peas

1½ cups Italian rice (see page 81)

2 to 4 cups good-quality vegetable broth

Salt

Freshly ground pepper

Freshly grated Parmigiano cheese

Warm the oil in a large saucepan over medium heat. Add the bacon, onion, carrot, parsley, and basil and sauté until the ingredients begin to color. Add the tomatoes, and cook, stirring, until some of the liquid evaporates and the sauce is thick.

Stir in the zucchini and peas. Cook over medium-high heat until the ingredients are almost tender and cooked down, then add the rice and proceed according to Risotto Basics (page 81), gradually ladling in the broth until the rice is tender; season to taste with salt and pepper, sprinkle with cheese, and serve.

Risotto di Ginevra

RISOTTO FROM GENEVA

I learned this recipe in Geneva and, lacking inspiration, I gave it the city's name.

FOR 6 SERVINGS

4 tablespoons olive, sunflower, or safflower oil

½ onion, minced

6 medium tomatoes, stem ends trimmed,
    cut in half

½ cup dry white wine

1½ cups Italian rice (see page 81)

Salt

Freshly ground pepper or paprika

4 tablespoons heavy cream or ½ cup plain yogurt

Freshly grated Parmigiano cheese

Pour the oil into a deep sauté pan, add the onion, and cook over medium heat, stirring, until the onions are lightly browned. Add the tomatoes and the wine. When the skins of the tomatoes crinkle, remove them. You may be able to do this while the tomatoes remain in the pan; or, if you like, remove the tomatoes from the pan, skin them over a dish to catch all their juices, then return tomatoes and juices to the pan.

Add the rice and stir it into the other ingredients for 1 minute. Add water to cover. Taste from time to time for doneness—if the water is absorbed before the rice is tender, add more in small amounts. When the rice is tender, stir well, add salt and pepper or paprika to

Risotto ai Asparagi e Formaggio

RISOTTO WITH ASPARAGUS AND CHEESE

2 pounds asparagus

Salt

4 to 5 tablespoons olive oil

1 medium onion, minced

1½ cups Italian rice (see page 81)

Freshly ground pepper

¼ pound Emmentaler or Swiss cheese, diced

Trim away the tough ends and wash the asparagus. Remove the tips, and cut the stalks into 1½-inch pieces. Bring a medium pot of water to a boil, add a pinch of salt, and drop in the stalks; cook for about 1 minute, then drop in the tips and cook for about 30 seconds longer. Drain the asparagus, reserving the cooking water, and refresh them quickly under cold water to stop the cooking.

Warm the oil in the pot over medium heat and add the onion; sauté, stirring, until it is softened but not browned. Add the rice and cook until it has turned opaque and the oil has been absorbed. Add salt to taste and a pinch of pepper.

Gradually add the reserved asparagus cooking water as described in Risotto Basics (page 81), until the rice is tender. Stir in the asparagus and the cheese. Stir the risotto once more in the pan. When the cheese begins to melt, the risotto is ready to be served.

Risotto ai Funghi
MUSHROOM RISOTTO

*D*ried mushrooms can be substituted for fresh ones, though you will have to reconstitute them by soaking them in water. Place them in about ½ cup tepid water for 20 to 30 minutes. Drain the mushrooms, reserving the soaking liquid. Dry the mushrooms on paper towels and wipe away any remaining grit. If you like, you can use the reserved liquid as part of the cooking liquid, which will intensify the mushroom taste.

FOR 6 SERVINGS

1 pound fresh mushrooms, a wild variety if possible,
    or a mixture of wild and white or 2 ounces dried
    porcini or other wild mushrooms (see above)

½ onion

1 clove garlic

3 or 4 fresh rosemary leaves

1 tablespoon fresh oregano leaves or 1 teaspoon dried

4 to 5 tablespoons olive oil

1 cup dry white wine

1½ cups Italian rice (see page 81)

Salt

Freshly ground pepper

½ cup heavy cream (optional)

¼ cup chopped fresh basil or Italian parsley

Dice the mushrooms together with the onion, garlic, rosemary, and oregano. Warm the oil in a medium saucepan over medium heat; add the diced mixture and sauté, stirring, for 3 to 5 minutes, until very lightly browned. Stir in the wine and let it cook until just about evaporated, then add the rice.

Stir the rice into the mixture for a minute or two until it becomes opaque. Add broth as described in Risotto Basics (page 81), until the rice is tender. Season to taste with salt and pepper. If you wish, remove the risotto from the heat and pour the cream over it, without stirring further. Turn the risotto out into a serving dish, sprinkle the basil over, and serve at once.

Risotto con Lenticchie

RISOTTO WITH LENTILS

This is a very easy dish to make, but the preparation begins a day in advance if you need to soak the lentils. Some varieties available today, such as the green lentils from France, do not require pre-soaking—check the directions on the package. You also need to pay attention to the cooking of the lentils; if they seem to be becoming tender quite quickly, cut the time so that they finish with the rice.

FOR 6 SERVINGS

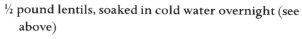

½ pound lentils, soaked in cold water overnight (see above)

2 tablespoons unsalted butter

1 medium onion, chopped

Handful of minced Italian parsley

4 cups or more good-quality chicken or vegetable broth

1½ cups Italian rice (see page 81)

Salt

Freshly ground pepper or paprika

Freshly grated Parmigiano cheese

Drain the lentils, place them in a fresh pot of water, bring to a boil, and cook until slightly underdone, 10 to 15 minutes. Drain again, reserving the cooking water.

Melt the butter in a large saucepan over medium heat, add the onion, and cook slowly, stirring, until the onion is very lightly browned; stir in the parsley. Add the lentils and 2 ladlesful of the broth and continue to cook for 10 minutes. Stir in the rice and gradually add more broth as described in Risotto Basics (page 81), until the lentils and rice reach the right point of doneness—tender, or *all'onda*, as we say in Italian, soft, but with enough body to leave a little wave when a spoon is passed through. Add salt to taste and serve with pepper and a dusting of cheese.

Risotto alla Milanese
Saffron-Flavored Risotto

For some, "risotto" and "Milanese" are practically synonymous, because this is without doubt the best known of all risotto preparations. Legend has it that in Milan's elegant past, Risotto Milanese was actually cooked in the entrances to boxes at the La Scala opera house, and then enjoyed right after the last ovation.

For 6 to 8 Servings

¼ teaspoon saffron threads

1 quart or more good-quality chicken broth

4 tablespoons unsalted butter

1 small onion, finely chopped

Marrow from one beef marrowbone (optional)

2 cups Italian rice (see page 81)

½ cup dry white wine (optional)

½ cup freshly grated Parmigiano cheese

Place the saffron threads in a small dish and cover with a tablespoon or so of warm water; set aside. Pour the broth into a medium-sized saucepan and bring it to a simmer. Melt the butter in a deep pot over medium heat. Following the method described in Risotto Basics (page 81), add the onion, marrow, and rice; add the wine and stir until it is absorbed. Gradually add the broth. Stir the saffron into the risotto toward the end of the cooking. When the rice is tender but still *al dente*, and the texture creamy, stir in the cheese and serve at once.

POLENTA BASICS

---

9 cups water

2 tablespoons salt

3 cups medium-grind Italian polenta
   or cornmeal (see Note)

Pour the water into a large heavy saucepan and bring it to a boil. Add the salt, lower the heat to medium, and gradually add the polenta by sprinkling it into the water from your hand, stirring the mixture constantly with a long-handled wooden spoon. Take care, and be patient as you add the polenta or it will be lumpy.

Continue to cook and stir the mixture constantly; if a lump does appear, try to crush it against the side of the pot. After about 30 minutes the polenta will be quite thick and will form large bubbles. The mixture is done when it begins to pull away from the side of the pot as you stir.

If you are serving the polenta soft, as with *Polenta al Parmigiano*, the polenta is ready to be finished according to the recipe.

If you are preparing a dish that calls for firm polenta, such as the *Polenta Crostini* (page 5) or *Polenta Pasticciata* (page 95), pour the mixture onto a large wooden board or work surface, baking sheet, or flat platter. Smooth the polenta with a wet spatula or your dampened hands, and shape it into a round or rectangle to the thickness specified in your recipe. The polenta will cool fairly rapidly and become firm enough to cut in 10 to 15 minutes. It can be made hours or even a day in advance and kept in the refrigerator.

MICROWAVE METHOD

Cooking polenta in a microwave oven will not save much overall cooking time, but it will liberate you from standing over the stove, stirring continually during the process. It also is a fairly fail-safe method, with less likelihood of lumping.

Place the polenta in a large microwave-safe bowl. Slowly add the water, stirring constantly with a fork until all the water is incorporated. Stir in the salt. Cover the bowl with a plate and place it into a microwave oven set on high. Cook the polenta for 10 minutes, remove the bowl, and stir to blend the mixture well (the polenta will begin to cook and thicken first along the side of the bowl). Cover the bowl again and return it to the oven for 10 minutes. Remove the bowl; if the polenta is not thick enough, stir again, cover, and cook for 2 to 5 minutes. Proceed as above.

NOTE: Of course, polenta *is* cornmeal, but the variety imported from Italy is meant specifically for making polenta dishes and will give them a more emphatic flavor and color.

Polenta al Parmigiano
POLENTA WITH PARMIGIANO

FOR 6 TO 8 SERVINGS

---

1 recipe soft Polenta (page 93)
1 cup unsalted butter
½ cup freshly grated Parmigiano cheese, plus
additional to serve

Prepare the polenta according to Polenta Basics (page 93). Melt the butter without letting it brown; stir the butter and the cheese into the polenta. Mix well to incorporate all the ingredients and serve at once. If you wish, additional cheese can be passed at the table.

Polenta Pasticciata
POLENTA WITH BUTTER AND CHEESE

I think polenta follows only pasta and rice in its versatility. You can create numerous variations on Polenta Pasticciata alone, adding or substituting other ingredients such as tomatoes, hard-boiled eggs, cooked ground meat, ham or prosciutto, and so on to the cheese layer. The choices are as rich as the taste and imagination of the cook.

FOR 6 SERVINGS

1 recipe Polenta (page 93)
6 tablespoons unsalted butter
1 pound thinly sliced semi-soft cheese
    such as Italian fontina

Prepare the polenta according to Polenta Basics (page 93). Pour the polenta onto a wooden board, marble slab, or large baking sheet to a thickness of ½ inch.

Preheat the oven to 375° F. Liberally butter a 9-by-12-inch baking dish. Melt the remaining butter.

When the polenta is completely cool and firm, cut it into slices ½ inch wide. Arrange a layer of polenta slices on the bottom of the baking dish. Cover the polenta with the cheese and pour some of the melted butter over. Continue to layer the polenta, cheese, and butter, until the ingredients are used up, finishing with a very lightly buttered layer of polenta.

Bake for 20 to 30 minutes, until the cheese is melted and the top is browned. At the table, cut the polenta into square servings.

In an Italian meal, meat is not so much the principal course as it is a second (secondo), but equal, course that follows pasta. The portions of meat are modest, and they are accompanied by vegetables and perhaps salad, or the salad may follow separately. Here you will find a number of simple and easy veal dishes that are very good for every day, a few traditional Neapolitan lamb dishes, and a handful from other regions.

Meat

Annibale, a beautiful butcher shop in Rome.

Vitello Arrosto
ROAST VEAL

4 to 5 tablespoons olive oil

Veal rump roast, 2 to 2½ pounds

3 medium onions, peeled and quartered

2 carrots, scraped and roughly chopped

1 branch celery, roughly chopped

Salt

Freshly ground pepper

½ cup good-quality vegetable, chicken, or veal broth

Warm the oil over medium heat in a flame-proof casserole or deep pot just large enough to hold the veal comfortably. Add the veal and brown it well on all sides; this will take 10 to 15 minutes.

Pour the broth into the pot and scrape up any browned bits stuck to the bottom. Add the onion, carrots, celery, and salt and pepper to taste. Cover the pot and lower the heat to keep the liquid at a simmer and cook for about 1 hour, turning the meat once during this time; add small amounts of broth or water if necessary to maintain the level of the liquid. Remove the meat to a platter. Press the contents of the pan through a strainer; spoon some of this sauce over the veal and pass the rest at the table.

Vitello alla Pizzaiola

VEAL COOKED IN THE MANNER OF THE PIZZA CHEF

Just imagine if, among my meat recipes, I made no reference to the pizza of my ancestors! Here, in fact, is a dish that brings to veal the characteristic flavor and aroma of the key ingredients of the classic pizza: tomatoes, garlic, parsley, and oregano. If you wish to have enough sauce for spaghetti to serve before or with the veal, increase the quantity of tomatoes by ½ pound.

FOR 4 TO 5 SERVINGS

4 to 5 tablespoons olive oil

2 cloves garlic, sliced

1¼ pound leg or shoulder of veal, sliced

Salt

Freshly ground pepper

1 generous pound fresh or canned tomatoes, seeded
  and chopped

Handful of chopped parsley

2 tablespoons chopped fresh oregano or 1 teaspoon dried

Heat the oil in a skillet large enough to hold the veal slices (or cook them in two batches). Add the garlic and cook over medium heat just until it begins to color. Season the veal slices with salt and pepper and add them to the pan. Cook the veal for about 2 minutes, turning a few times; take care not to overcook or keep the heat too high or the meat will toughen.

Remove the meat to a plate and cover to keep it warm. Put the tomatoes, most of the parsley, and the oregano into the pan. Lower the heat and cook the mixture, stirring from time to time, for about 15 minutes, until the sauce has thickened. Return the meat and any juices that have gathered around it to the pan; add salt and pepper to taste. Cook the veal in the sauce over medium heat for about 1 minute, just enough to heat it through. Sprinkle on the remaining parsley and serve immediately.

Spezzatino di Vitello
VEAL STEW

This dish, as the preceding roast veal and the one to follow for meatballs, was inspired by that incomparable cook, my sister, Maria. I stay with her on my brief visits to Rome and my mouth always waters in anticipation of what she'll bring to the table. Maria coyly remarks while serving me her various offerings, "I've made these for you because I didn't think you knew how to prepare them." It's a game, but one full of family affection and perhaps the only one that can deflate my vanity.

FOR 4 TO 5 SERVINGS

2 to 3 tablespoons olive oil

2 pounds veal stew meat, cut into 2-inch cubes

1 clove garlic, minced

1 tablespoon minced fresh rosemary leaves or 1 teaspoon dried, crumbled

½ cup dry white wine

1 cup good-quality chicken or veal broth

With Mamma and little Maria at our grandfather's house in Pozzuoli. There was a small garden, quite wild with two trees, one apple and one apricot. To us it was the Garden of Eden, the enchanted place of our childhood.

Heat the oil in a pan large enough to hold the meat. Add the meat and cook over medium heat until it is browned on all sides; add the garlic and rosemary and pour in the wine. Cook over high heat until the wine has evaporated. Add the broth, lower the heat, cover the pan, and simmer for about 1 hour, until the meat is fork tender.

MY SISTER MARIA

I confess: I'm quite proud of my skill in the kitchen. And in a contest with other cooks, I'd be hard pressed to concede that any were better than me. After writing my first cookbook, I was honored by one of Italy's most prestigious gastronomic societies. They gave a party and awarded me a certificate proclaiming me a member. For me, it was like receiving the Academy Award for cuisine, and I include it among my life's most cherished tributes. I don't mention this to boast, but as an honest prelude to admitting that my sister, Maria, is an even better cook than me. Maria is the mother of two daughters and already a young grandmother of three, and her time in the kitchen is spent, not only out of the necessity to feed so many, but in response to what I would call a natural vocation for the stove. Grandmother Luisa's bravura has been passed down to us both, but to Maria in a more complete and profound way. Sometimes when I'm with her, we wonder if from on high, Nonna Luisa still guides us, approving of us and pleased with how we cook.

Maria and I are proud of our new dresses in this photograph taken by an American GI. I was 11, Maria was 7 years old.

A visit with Maria during the shooting of Two Women. *Photo by Alfred Eisenstaedt.*

Piatto di Carne Rustica

COUNTRY-STYLE MEAT

FOR 4 SERVINGS

1 medium onion

6 to 7 tablespoons olive oil

½ cup black olives, pitted and roughly chopped or
sliced

2 tablespoons drained capers

1 pound thinly sliced veal

Bread crumbs

Slice the onion into very thin rounds and place them, with 5 tablespoons oil, the olives, and capers in a deep platter or wide, shallow bowl. Add the veal slices, turn them over several times in the mixture, and let them marinate for about 1 hour.

Pat the excess moisture from the veal slices, then dredge them in the bread crumbs. Heat 1 to 2 tablespoons oil in a large skillet over medium-high heat. Add the veal slices and cook until they are nicely browned on both sides, about 2 minutes total—do not overcook the meat.

Remove the veal to a serving platter. Drain the marinade ingredients and place them in the pan, lower the heat, and cook, stirring occasionally, until the onion is soft but not browned, 5 to 10 minutes longer. Return the meat to the pan to heat briefly, then serve.

FROM LEFT:
Piatto di Carne Rustica, Saltimbocca,
and Piccatina di Vitello *in preparation.*

Saltimbocca

SAUTÉED VEAL WITH PROSCIUTTO AND SAGE

This delightful dish never loses its popularity. As most people know by now, the name means "jumps in the mouth"—because it is so good. This is simple to prepare, but, like so many simple dishes, its goodness depends on the quality of the ingredients used, so use the best veal you can find, and imported Italian prosciutto.

FOR 4 SERVINGS

1 pound thinly sliced veal
¼ pound thinly sliced prosciutto
Fresh sage leaves
5 tablespoons olive oil
½ cup dry white wine

Place 1 or 2 sage leaves on each veal slice. Place pieces of prosciutto over the sage leaves; secure the layers with toothpicks, as shown in the photograph on the previous page.

Heat the oil in a pan over medium-high heat. Add the meat packets, veal side down, and cook until nicely browned, a minute or so, then turn and cook until the prosciutto is golden brown; take care not to overcook the meat. Pour the wine into the pan and scrape up any browned bits stuck to the bottom; cook until the wine is evaporated. Place the meat on a platter, drizzle the pan juices over, and serve immediately.

Piccatina di Vitello

Sautéed Veal with Lemon

This is another of those quick veal dishes that are so easy to prepare on a daily basis, no matter how busy you may be. This one is ready, start to finish, in 10 to 15 minutes.

For 4 Servings

5 tablespoons olive oil

1 tablespoon all-purpose flour

4 tablespoons good-quality chicken or veal broth

1 pound thinly sliced veal

Juice of 1 lemon

¼ cup minced Italian parsley

Place the oil in a skillet over medium heat; add the flour and stir to combine. Stir in the broth and whisk to combine and smooth the mixture. Place the veal slices in the pan and keep turning them in the thick sauce until they are cooked through and tender, about 3 minutes. Pour in the lemon juice, stir to combine, and sprinkle the parsley over. Serve immediately.

ABOVE: *Carlo Jr. meets his newly born brother,*
Edoardo, in 1973 as their father looks on.
OPPOSITE: *Jean Barthet, the famous French designer,*
who always created fabulous hats for me, made this
composition illustration of the boys.

Polpette di Livia

MEAT PATTIES

Every year at Christmas my family and most intimate friends gather in Geneva, the city where my sons were born and spent their earliest years. Geneva is also the city of an unforgettable friend who is no longer with us, Dr. Hubert Watteville, the great medical genius who, when all else and a host of other doctors had failed, gave me the great joy of motherhood. It seems natural that we are in Geneva at the time of the year when emotions run high and family ties are celebrated.

Before leaving California or wherever in the world they may be, Carlo Jr. and Edoardo are always eager to know if our longtime cook, Livia, now eighty-four, will be with us. Once reassured, my sons begin to anticipate the gastronomic treats that await them. For them, Livia's most enticing dish is her meatballs, Le Polpette di Livia. There is no dish that they crave more, and once the little meatballs in their tasty sauce appear on the table, they devour more than their fair share.

FOR 4 SERVINGS

1½ cups milk

4 small pieces stale or lightly toasted bread, crusts removed

1 pound twice-ground beef or veal

Salt

Freshly ground pepper

Flour for dredging

Safflower or light olive oil

½ cup dry white wine

¼ cup good-quality chicken broth

1 cup heavy cream

(continued)

Pour the milk in a bowl and add the bread; set aside to allow the bread to soften completely. Squeeze the excess moisture from the bread and place it in a mixing bowl; add the meat and salt and pepper to taste. Stir to combine the ingredients well, and with your hands, shape the mixture into meatballs about 2 inches in diameter. Dredge the meatballs in the flour, then flatten them slightly to form chubby little patties.

Pour about ¼ inch of oil into a medium-sized skillet over medium heat. When the oil is hot, add the meatballs and sauté on both sides until they are golden brown. Remove the meatballs from the skillet and place them on paper towels to drain. Pour off the excess oil from the skillet, add the wine, and cook over medium-high heat, stirring and scraping up any browned bits stuck to the bottom of the skillet.

When most of the wine has evaporated, add the chicken broth and cream and cook just to warm—do not let the mixture boil. Return the patties to the pan and cook for 1 to 2 minutes, just long enough to heat through and absorb the flavors of the sauce. Remove from the heat at once and serve.

Carlo Jr. and Edoardo.

Polpette di Carne

MEATBALLS

FOR 4 TO 5 SERVINGS

½ pound fresh white bread crumbs

1 cup milk

1 pound ground beef or veal

¼ cup freshly grated Parmigiano cheese

2 large eggs

Handful of minced Italian parsley

Salt

Freshly ground pepper

1 cup (or more) dry bread crumbs

Olive oil

Place the bread crumbs in a bowl with the milk and let them soak for about 30 minutes. Squeeze out any excess milk and combine the bread crumbs with the meat, cheese, eggs, parsley, and salt and pepper to taste; stir or use your hands to produce a smooth, uniform mixture. Form the mixture into small meatballs, then roll them in the bread crumbs. Heat just enough oil in a sauté pan to cover the bottom. When the oil is hot, add the meatballs and cook over medium heat, turning the meatballs to color them golden brown all over; add additional oil in small amounts, as needed. Remove the meatballs to paper towels to drain, then serve hot.

Meat hooks in an elegant butcher shop in Rome.

Filetto alla Griglia

GRILLED CHÂTEAUBRIAND

A few years ago I was shooting a film in Rome and was invited to lunch by a journalist and his wife. The woman was as unpleasant and affected as her husband was agreeable. I ordered grilled fillet of beef. The journalist's wife, trying to appear casual and yet quite correct, ordered "Châteaubriand." When they arrived, our orders were, of course, identical. She called the waiter back and, again trying to seem casual, said to him, "But I ordered Châteaubriand." And the waiter replied, "That's what I'm serving you—the center cut of a fillet of beef." I can't describe the mortification that she obviously felt, the amused smile of her husband, and my own efforts to suppress an outburst of laughter.

By any name, this is an excellent cut of beef to season in a simple marinade and cook over a charcoal fire. Serve it with grilled vegetables for an elegant but easy summer dinner. Châteaubriands vary in size, so consult your butcher regarding the amount you will need.

FOR 4 SERVINGS

Center cut from a fillet of beef (about 2 pounds)

¼ cup olive oil

1 clove garlic, roughly chopped

1 tablespoon red wine vinegar

Leaves from a sprig of rosemary

Freshly ground pepper

Salt

The night before you plan to serve it, wipe the meat thoroughly with paper towels and place it in a glass or porcelain dish. Whisk together the remaining ingredients and brush them over the meat. Cover the dish with plastic wrap and place in the refrigerator; turn the meat from time to time.

When you are ready to cook, remove the meat from the refrigerator and prepare a charcoal fire. Drain the steak of excess marinade, and, when the fire is ready, place it on the grill; cook the meat, turning it on all sides, until it is nicely charred all over but still rare or medium rare within, about 15 minutes.

Il Carpaccio

Vittorio Carpaccio was a magnificent 15th-century Venetian painter. His canvases were enormous and densely covered with grand backgrounds and motifs. Hundreds of years later, the artist's name was given to this dish when it was first introduced at Harry's Bar in Venice. Carpaccio could probably have imagined anything except that his name would become attached to a quintessentially simple recipe that is known around the world. In fact, the most challenging part is cutting the beef into very thin slices, as you would prosciutto. For best results, ask your butcher to do that for you.

FOR 4 TO 6 SERVINGS

2 pounds lean beef, very thinly sliced across the grain
1 cup olive oil
Juice of 1 lemon
¼ cup minced Italian parsley
Salt
Freshly ground pepper

Divide the slices of beef among individual plates, then drizzle the oil over, sprinkle with the lemon juice and parsley, and season with salt and pepper. Nothing else is needed to have the satisfaction of preparing a very refined dish in just a few minutes.

Agnello Bella Napoli

LAMB FROM BEAUTIFUL NAPLES

This dish, sometimes called Agnello al Forno, *is a typical, popular Neapolitan dish, a shining example of traditional home cooking. It is sometimes made with goat, though less frequently now than in the past. In and around Naples, the amount of oil used may be significantly more than the amount here and can be increased according to your preference.*

FOR 6 SERVINGS

2 pounds cubed lamb stew meat, such as from
the shoulder

3 to 4 medium onions, peeled and quartered

2 pounds all-purpose potatoes, peeled and cut into
chunks, or new potatoes, halved or quartered

2 cloves garlic, crushed

¼ cup minced Italian parsley

½ cup minced fresh basil

2 tablespoons fresh oregano leaves
or 2 teaspoons dried

Salt

Freshly ground pepper

2 pounds ripe but firm tomatoes, roughly chopped

1 to 2 tablespoons unsalted butter (optional)

4 tablespoons olive oil

Preheat the oven to 350° F. Butter a large baking dish. Wipe the lamb chunks on paper towels and place them in the dish; add the onions, potatoes, and garlic. Sprinkle over the parsley, basil, oregano, and salt and pepper. Top with the chopped tomato and a few small pieces of butter. Drizzle the olive oil over all. Bake for about 1½ hours, until the lamb is fork tender and the potatoes are cooked through.

FOLLOWING PAGES:
*Naples' magnificent
Piazza del Plebiscito.*

Agnello Ubriaco

Drunken Lamb

To be honest, I like this dish, which is usually found in the homes of simple country people, not only for its goodness, but also for the hint of gaiety that the word ubriaco—*drunken*—*gives it.*

For 6 Servings

6 loin or rib lamb chops

1 lamb shoulder, cut into medium-sized chunks

1 tablespoon olive oil

4 slices bacon, roughly chopped

1 large onion, diced

Salt

Freshly ground pepper

1 (750-ml) bottle dry red wine

1 branch celery, coarsely chopped

1 clove garlic, crushed

1 tablespoon fresh rosemary leaves, minced

1 tablespoon drained capers (optional)

Wipe the lamb chops and pieces of shoulder with paper towels. Heat the oil in a deep pot or flame-proof casserole over medium heat; add the meat and brown it well all over. Remove the meat, add the bacon and onion, and sauté until the onion is golden. Return the lamb to the pan, sprinkle on a little salt and pepper, and pour in the wine. Add the celery, garlic, rosemary, and capers. Cover the pot and cook over medium-low heat, to maintain a lively simmer, for 1 hour, then uncover and continue cooking until the liquid is almost completely evaporated. Taste for doneness—the meat should be fork tender and the sauce quite thick; adjust the seasoning as necessary with salt and pepper, and serve.

Agnello al Forno
ROASTED LEG OF LAMB

There are exceptions, but all over Italy, roasted lamb is the meat of choice for Easter and for other Spring dinners. This preparation is typically simple—the meat needs nothing more than garlic and rosemary to enhance its own sweet, rich flavors.

FOR 8 TO 10 SERVINGS

1 (6- to 7-pound) semi-boneless leg of lamb, tied with string

2 cloves garlic, cut into slivers

6 long sprigs rosemary

1 tablespoon coarse salt

2 teaspoons freshly ground pepper

Additional rosemary for the platter (optional)

Preheat the oven to 400° F.

Using a knife with a very slender tip, make incisions randomly all over the meat. As you make an incision, push a sliver of garlic into the hole. Tuck the sprigs of rosemary under the strings and sprinkle the meat with salt and pepper all over.

Place the lamb on the rack of a roasting pan and roast it until you can hear the fat sizzle, 15 to 20 minutes. Lower the oven temperature to 350° F. and cook for 1 hour, or until the internal temperature reaches 140° F. Remove the roast from the oven and let it rest, covered with aluminum foil, for 15 minutes before carving. Serve the lamb on a bed of rosemary.

What's dinner without flowers, especially on holidays? In Italy on the Sunday before Easter— Palm Sunday—we used to decorate the house with small olive branches and braided strips of palm leaves. On Easter, lilies are traditional, along with any other flowers that signal Spring.
FOLLOWING PAGES:
Agnello al Forno.

Pollo alla Porchetta

CHICKEN ROASTED AS PORK

This is a dish that I encountered in Romagna during the shooting of Boccaccio '70. *The inspiration, however, is Rome, where a young pig is stuffed with herbs before roasting. It is a succulent, incredibly tasty preparation and I was amazed that a roasted chicken could taste so much like pork.*

If you like, fennel and garlic cloves roasted along with the bird are excellent accompaniments.

FOR 4 SERVINGS

1 (3½-pound) chicken

1 cup minced ham

Giblets from the chicken, minced (optional)

Leaves from a sprig of rosemary, minced

1 sprig of the feathery top of a fennel bulb, minced

1 clove garlic, minced

1 tablespoon olive oil, plus additional

Salt

Freshly ground pepper

1 medium fennel bulb, cut into 6 wedges (optional)

1 head garlic, cloves separated but not peeled
   (optional)

Preheat the oven to 375° F. Wash the chicken thoroughly inside and out and remove any excess fat. Pat the chicken dry with paper towels.

Combine the ham, giblets, rosemary, fennel top, garlic, 1 tablespoon oil, and pinches of salt and pepper. Fill the cavity of the chicken with the mixture. Lightly oil a small roasting pan and place the chicken in it; brush a bit of oil over the chicken. If you are using them, place the wedges of fennel around the chicken and lightly brush them with oil, then scatter the garlic cloves around. Roast for 1 hour and 15 minutes, or until the skin is golden brown and the juices that run from the thigh joint are clear.

Cappone Emiliano
STUFFED CAPON IN THE EMILIA STYLE

Emilia is the western half of Emilia-Romagna in north central Italy, a region so notable for its cuisine that it is the one all other Italians take pride in outside their own. The food of Emilia-Romagna is noted for its richness and refinement, making it a true alta cucina.

This recipe was prepared in my Geneva kitchen one day by a friend from Emilia who divides his time between literature and gastronomy, of which he is a great student.

If it's hard for you to find capon in the market, you can substitute a large roasting chicken, in which case the stuffing quantity may be a bit more than you need. This is a dish for a special occasion, and requires a bit of time to prepare, but if you have your butcher bone the bird, the rest will be relatively easy. In any case, all can be done in advance. If you would like to serve Cappone Emiliano *with a sauce,* Pesto Genovese *(page 72) or* Salsa Sophia *(page 70) are good choices.*

Claudio Volpetti at Testaccio, one of Rome's specialty food shops.

1 (7- to 8-pound) capon, boned, except for the legs

2 tablespoons olive oil

¾ pound ground pork

¾ pound ground veal

4 ounces boiled ham, minced

4 ounces prosciutto, minced

½ cup Marsala wine

3 eggs

Salt

Freshly ground pepper

Milk, if needed

Preheat the oven to 350° F.

Rinse the capon well inside and out and pat it dry with paper towels. Warm the oil in a medium-sized skillet over medium heat. Add the pork and veal, and stir until the meat begins to lose its color.

Turn the meat mixture out into a bowl and stir in the ham, prosciutto, eggs, wine, and pinches of salt and pepper. If the mixture is too dense, it can be lightened by stirring in a little milk. Stuff the capon with the mixture, but do not pack it too tightly. Truss the opening and roast for about 1 hour or until the juices run clear.

Let the capon rest for 15 minutes, then slice it and serve. Pass the sauce, if you are using one, at the table.

Coniglio alle Erbe

RABBIT WITH HERBS

FOR 4 SERVINGS

1 (3-pound) rabbit, cut into pieces

½ cup white wine vinegar

Olive oil, as needed

4 ounces pancetta or bacon, minced

2 small onions, diced

2 carrots, scraped and diced

1 branch celery, diced

2 to 3 sage leaves, minced

2 to 3 sprigs rosemary, minced

Flour for dredging

½ cup dry white wine

Salt

Freshly ground pepper

¼ cup drained capers

Place the rabbit pieces in a shallow dish and pour the vinegar over; add water to just cover and set aside to marinate for 1 hour. Warm about 1 tablespoon oil in a large skillet or sauté pan over medium heat. Add the pancetta and sauté briefly; add the onions, carrots, celery, and the herbs, and cook, stirring, until the ingredients are soft.

Remove the rabbit pieces from the marinade and pat them dry with paper towels. Dredge the rabbit pieces in the flour and add them to the pan; raise the heat slightly and sauté until nicely browned all over. Add the wine and salt and pepper to taste. Partially cover the pan, lower the heat, and cook slowly until the rabbit is tender, about 1 hour, adding a little water if the pan begins to seem dry. When the rabbit is cooked, add the capers and cook for about 3 more minutes, then serve.

The world of the kitchen is like that of finance. A good cook must approach food like a broker faced with various financial options, making choices and maximizing the advantages. With fish the work begins at the market because it is essential to choose the product yourself, evaluating its freshness, its origin, and final destination in the kitchen. Examine the eyes and gills first; the eyes must be bright and clear, the gills red. Look also for firm flesh, and if you are at all uncertain don't risk turning out an inedible dish. Shellfish likewise should be bright and lively; lobsters of course must be bought while still alive, clams and mussels with tightly closed shells. One of the best pieces of advice I can give you is to find a good fishmonger and support him by becoming a loyal customer.

Fish

The most demanding Neapolitans go to the market first thing in the morning to buy fish caught the night before. When we moved to Rome, my mother cooked fish only when an uncle or friend would bring it from our native Pozzuoli.

BACCALÀ BASICS

Baccalà, *salt-preserved codfish, is one of those economical foods that the genius of poor people has transformed into a near delicacy. Like many such staples,* baccalà *is versatile, which makes it one of the outstanding items of the* cucina povera. *Today it has transcended its category and is cooked and enjoyed for its own sake, with no sense of deprivation.* Baccalà *can be found in endless preparations throughout Italy, particularly in the Veneto, around Naples and Rome, and in Tuscany, often on the menus of expensive restaurants.*

Because it is preserved in salt, traditional baccalà *requires soaking in water—many changes of water—over a period of two or three days before it can be used, in order to remove excess salt and soften the flesh. Today, however, it is easy to find good-quality* baccalà *presoaked, which means it needs only a day or so of additional soaking; at some fishmongers you can eliminate even this step by getting* baccalà *ready for its final preparation. In any event, it must be prepared with care in order to make it tender and remove the excess salt. If you buy* baccalà *completely prepared, be sure to get thick center pieces and avoid the flat sections near the tail. If you do buy* baccalà *that has not already been prepared, simply soak it for at least two days in a large container of cool water and change the water several times each day. Cut the fish according to your recipe, remove the bones, and drain it well on a towel.*

Baccalà in Insalata
COLD SALT COD WITH CAULIFLOWER

FOR 4 SERVINGS

2 pounds *baccalà* in fairly large pieces, soaked
   (see page 131)

½ cup olive oil

1 lemon, sliced

Salt

1 head cauliflower, separated into flowerets

½ cup green olives, pitted and minced

1 tablespoon red wine vinegar

Freshly ground pepper

Handful of minced Italian parsley

Place the salt cod in a deep skillet or sauté pan, add 1 tablespoon oil, a thin slice of lemon, and enough water to just barely cover. Bring the water to a gentle boil, lower the heat slightly, and simmer for 2 minutes. Turn off the heat and let the fish cool to room temperature in the water.

Meanwhile, bring a large pot of water to a boil; add a large pinch of salt and drop in the cauliflower. When the cauliflower is *al dente*, drain and refresh it under cold water. Remove the fish from the cooking water and drain it well on paper towels. Cut the fish into large cubes and arrange them on a deep platter or shallow bowl with the olives and the cauliflower. Whisk together the remaining oil, the vinegar, and pepper to taste, and pour the dressing over the salad; sprinkle the parsley over and arrange the remaining lemon slices around the dish.

VARIATION: Omit the cauliflower and substitute 3 cups cherry tomatoes, cut in half, and 2 stalks celery with their leaves, trimmed and thinly sliced; black olives can be substituted for the green ones.

Baccalà ai Ferri

GRILLED SALT COD

T̵his is the way we used to prepare baccalà *at home when I was a child. It is very simple and delicious, but much better if you use a charcoal grill. A really good olive oil also makes a difference.*

FOR 4 SERVINGS

2 pounds large pieces *baccalà*, soaked and drained
   (see page 131)

½ cup extra-virgin olive oil

1 clove garlic, finely minced

2 tablespoons fresh rosemary leaves, finely minced

Lemon wedges

Prepare a charcoal fire. When the fire is ready, lightly brush the pieces of fish with some of the olive oil and place them on the grill. Turn the pieces, taking care not to break them up, so that they cook evenly on all sides. The *baccalà* needs only to acquire color and the light, smoky flavor of the coals as it heats through.

Meanwhile, combine the remaining oil with the garlic and rosemary. When the fish is ready, place it on a platter, drizzle the oil mixture over, and serve with the lemon wedges.

Beauty contests were popular and frequent when I was a young woman. Here I am, at the age of 15 with other eager contestants in a pageant in the town of Salsomaggiore.

Tonno Fresco con Funghi

FRESH TUNA WITH MUSHROOMS

FOR 4 SERVINGS

1 ounce dried mushrooms

4 tablespoons olive oil

6 anchovy fillets, drained

2 to 3 cloves garlic, minced

1 cup dry white wine

4 fresh tuna steaks (about 2 pounds total)

2 tablespoons chopped Italian parsley

Salt

Freshly ground pepper

½ teaspoon freshly grated nutmeg

4 tablespoons unsalted butter

Juice of ½ lemon

Place the mushrooms in a small bowl, cover them with tepid water, and set them aside to reconstitute for 15 minutes.

Drain the mushrooms, pat them dry, and chop them. Heat the oil in a large skillet or sauté pan and add the mushrooms, anchovies, and garlic; cook, stirring, until the anchovies have dissolved in the oil. Pour in the wine and bring the mixture just to a boil; lower the heat and continue cooking to reduce the liquid slightly, then place the tuna steaks in the pan. Cook the steaks on both sides, for a total of about 5 minutes; sprinkle with the parsley, salt and pepper to taste, and the nutmeg.

When the tuna is cooked, remove it from the pan with a slotted spatula to a heated serving platter. Add the butter to the sauce in the pan and whisk to incorporate it well. Whisk in the lemon juice. Pour the sauce over the tuna steaks and serve at once.

NOTE: A quarter-pound of fresh wild or white mushrooms can be substituted for the dried; add them at the same point.

Filetti di Sogliola con Salsa all'Uovo

FILLET OF SOLE IN MARSALA SAUCE

If you can find fresh Dover sole or grey sole, it will be worth a bit of extravagance for this elegant preparation. The fish is simply sautéed, while the sauce provides a rich, satiny counterpoint.

FOR 4 SERVINGS

2 pounds sole fillets (about 12 small fillets)

Flour for dredging

4 tablespoons unsalted butter

6 egg yolks

1 cup Marsala wine or dry Sherry

Salt

Freshly ground pepper

Pat the sole fillets dry with paper towels. Dredge the fillets in the flour, coating them lightly but evenly on both sides. Heat the butter in a large skillet over medium heat; when the foam subsides, carefully add the fillets to the pan and cook them until they are lightly golden brown on one side.

Beat the egg yolks together with the wine and pinches of salt and pepper, until well blended. Turn the fillets and cook for about 1 minute, then lower the heat and pour the egg mixture over. Cook for 3 minutes and serve immediately.

Sardines a Beccafico

STUFFED SARDINES

This Sicilian dish takes its name from a preparation also used for small birds. Sardines are wonderful, whether fried, grilled, or baked, but I think that this is my favorite way of all.

FOR 4 SERVINGS

1 pound fresh sardines

6 tablespoons olive oil

6 tablespoons fresh bread crumbs

1 tablespoon raisins

1 tablespoon pinoli

¼ cup chopped Italian parsley

2 anchovy fillets, drained and chopped

Freshly ground pepper

Preheat the oven to 350° F.

Wash the sardines and slit them lengthwise through the bellies without cutting through the back skin; lay them out flat and remove the heads and the backbone (you can ask your fishmonger to do this). Let the sardines drain on paper towels while you prepare the stuffing.

Heat 4 tablespoons oil in a medium-sized skillet. Add 4 tablespoons bread crumbs and cook them, stirring, until they are crisp but not burned. Turn the bread crumbs into a mixing bowl and gently combine them with the remaining ingredients, adding pepper to taste.

Divide the bread mixture among the sardines, spreading it over the flesh. Then, starting at the tail end, roll up each sardine and secure it closed with a toothpick. Use some of the remaining oil to generously coat a baking dish. Place the sardines in the dish, drizzle over the remaining oil, and sprinkle with the remaining bread crumbs. Bake for about 30 minutes.

Roast Fish alla Fiamma

FLAMED ROAST FISH

I came across this interesting way of preparing whole fish on a visit to the coast of Sardinia. You can do this with a large fish or with individual small fish. The fish can be baked in an oven at high heat, but for really superb results a charcoal fire is best. To me, this dish is magic. Besides the bed and blanket of herbs you can stuff a sprig or two into the fish's cavity before roasting.

FOR 4 SERVINGS

1 (2- to 3-pound) whole fish such as striped bass or
    red snapper, or 4 (1-pound) fish such as porgy or
    butterfish

2 tablespoons olive oil

Coarse salt, preferably sea salt

Abundant sprigs of mixed fresh herbs such as
    rosemary, thyme, parsley, and fennel tops

½ cup cognac

Prepare a charcoal fire.

Clean the fish and dry it well. When the fire is ready, brush the fish with the olive oil and place it on the grill; if you have a basket for grilling fish, use it. If you have a covered grill, the fish can be cooked without turning; if not, turn the fish to roast it on both sides. The fish will take about 20 minutes to cook through, depending on its size and the heat of your fire. Check for doneness by inspecting the flesh around the backbone; the fish is cooked if there is no sign of blood.

Meanwhile, spread a layer of salt on a platter large enough to hold the fish; cover with half the herbs. Warm the cognac. Place the grilled fish on the herbs and cover it completely with the remaining herbs. Quickly pour the cognac over the fish, ignite it, and let the flames burn out. Brush the burned herbs aside and serve the fish immediately.

Spigola di Natale

CHRISTMAS BASS

My cook, Livia, has, for several years without fail, come to my home in Geneva for Christmas. I love her dearly because she has shared so much with my family. She was with us when we lived in the Roman countryside, and has known my sons since they were born. Livia is an extraordinary person— she was eighty-four this year and remains as alert and lively as a young girl. When I look at Livia it seems as if the years haven't passed at all, and this feeling is even more vivid when tasting her food. She prepares traditional Christmas fare, including fish on Christmas Eve. You cannot imagine her rigor as she dedicates herself to preparing the beautiful stuffed and decorated striped bass. I wish that time could stand still and that for many years to come, my Christmas holidays would find our dear Livia with us in Geneva.

FOR 8 SERVINGS

1 whole striped bass weighing 5 to 6 pounds, cleaned

Salt

1 lemon, quartered

4 sprigs Italian parsley

4 medium potatoes, boiled

4 cooked carrots

½ cup green olives, pitted

¾ pound fresh peas or 10 ounces frozen peas, cooked

¼ cup minced Italian parsley

Freshly ground pepper

About 1 cup homemade or good-quality store-
    bought mayonnaise (recipe follows)

2 hard-boiled eggs

To decorate: 2 carrots , and 2 lemons or 2 seedless
    cucumbers, very thinly sliced

Pour enough water to cover the fish into a fish poacher or large roasting pan (if you are not using a poacher with a tray, wrap the fish in cheesecloth, which will help you lift it out later). Bring the water just to a low boil, add a large pinch of salt, the lemon, and parsley sprigs. Lower the bass into the water, cover, and lower the heat to maintain a gentle simmer. Simmer until the fish is cooked through, about 40 minutes; it should not show signs of blood in the flesh around the bones.

Carefully lift the fish out of the poaching liquid and set it on a platter to cool to room temperature. While the fish is cooling, prepare the filling (which is essentially an *insalata russa*, or Russian salad). Cut the potatoes and the carrots into small cubes and chop the olives. Place them in a bowl and add the peas, the minced parsley, and salt and pepper to taste. Gently stir in enough mayonnaise to hold the filling together.

Cut off and set aside the head and tail of the bass. Split the bass open lengthwise and carefully remove the skeleton by lifting it off the underside of the fish (a blunt knife such as a boning knife can help). Place the underside of the fish on a long serving platter and spread the filling over it (excess filling can be served as a salad at the table). Lay the top half of the fish over the filling and remove the skin. Reposition the head and tail. Coat the body of the bass with mayonnaise and garnish with carrots and lemons or cucumbers in a pattern resembling fish scales.

I prefer pure white table linens, embroidered or edged in some way. In Geneva, I store them in a beautiful antique chest in my dining room. On less formal tables, a small garden table, for instance, you can use cloth place mats, especially at breakfast or lunch.

FOLLOWING PAGES:
Livia's decorated bass is the centerpiece of our Christmas Eve dinner. A dear friend of mine who lives in Paris sends me a magnificent azalea plant every year that is always part of our holiday decoration.

Maionese

MAYONNAISE

Mayonnaise is easy to make at home if you take care and do not try to rush the process. You just need to be careful about mayonnaise pazza*—crazy mayonnaise—when the ingredients just don't amalgamate, or separate after they do. My advice is to beat the ingredients well, with a lot of energy and without stopping, and above all to add the oil to the egg mixture very, very slowly.*

FOR ABOUT 1 CUP

2 egg yolks
1 tablespoon dried mustard
Salt
Freshly ground white pepper
1 cup vegetable oil
1 teaspoon lemon juice

Place the egg yolk, mustard, and pinches of salt and pepper in a large, chilled bowl. Beat with an electric mixer or whisk energetically to combine well. Gradually add the oil, drop by drop, whisking constantly, until the mixture is smooth and emulsified. Continue pouring in the oil very slowly, in a thin stream, until it is all incorporated. Stir in the lemon juice. Store the mayonnaise in the refrigerator.

RIGHT: *A serving of* Spigola di Natale.

Spiedini alla Marinara

GRILLED SEAFOOD ON SKEWERS

The variety of spiedini—skewered meat or other ingredients—is almost endless; spiedini seem to come in every imaginable form. Spiedini of seafood can be particularly successful, tasty and easy to prepare. The most important aspects are good fresh fish and a nice, hot charcoal fire—although broiled spiedini are almost as good. Choose an assortment of fish from those listed below or others that look especially appealing when you go to the fish market.

FOR **4** TO **6** SERVINGS

2 to 2½ total pounds seafood such as: calamaretti or small calamari, jumbo shrimp or prawns (with heads on if possible), *orata* (porgy) or other firm-fleshed white fish, and cooked octopus

2 tablespoons olive oil

1 clove garlic, crushed

2 tablespoons chopped Italian parsley

2 lemons, cut into wedges

Prepare a charcoal fire.

Clean the seafood carefully, but do not shell the shrimp. Cut the fish and the octopus into 2-inch pieces—everything should be about the same size. In a small pan, warm the olive oil and cook the garlic until it is lightly browned; remove from the heat and add the parsley.

Alternating the types, thread the seafood onto individual skewers. Brush the seafood with the oil mixture and place the skewers on the grill. Cook the fish quickly, close to the fire, for 1 to 3 minutes on each side—just enough to cook through and absorb the smoky taste of the fire without losing the tang of the sea. Serve with the lemon wedges.

Aragosta al Rum

LOBSTER WITH RUM

Lobster is one of the most prized of all seafood. It can be prepared in many ways, but success is always dependent on starting with lobsters that are not merely alive but lively and then preparing them with care. Last year, while shooting my latest film, Le Soleil *in Casablanca, some members of the crew asked me to supper in an inexpensive restaurant in the port "where you can taste the best lobster in the world." I accepted their invitiation, not only for the lobster but because stage hands and electricians are always my dearest colleagues on a set. It was a great evening, and the dish, which I share with you here, also was great. Lobsters from off the Moroccan coast are renowned, and that evening, thanks to some simple creativity on the part of the cook, they lived up to their reputation.*

FOR EACH SERVING

1 live lobster, 1 to 1½ pounds
2 tablespoons unsalted butter, melted
1 tablespoon rum

Prepare a charcoal fire.

Bring a large pot of water to a boil. Drop in the lobsters and, when the water returns to a boil, cook for 8 to 10 minutes, depending on how many are in the pot. Remove the lobsters from the water, place them on a cutting board, and cut them in half lengthwise.

When the fire is ready, place the lobster halves, shell side down, on the grill. Grill, basting the flesh with the butter, for about 5 minutes. Place the lobsters on a serving platter, pour on the rum, ignite, and serve as soon as the flames die out.

A scene from Scandal in Sorrento, *1955, which also starred Vittorio De Sica. That film was like a course at a university of fish cooking. Besides the beauty of the landscape, the region is famous for its fishermen and the richness and variety of their catch.*

In the Italian kitchen, vegetables hold a position of importance second only to pasta. Often they are prepared with pristine simplicity in ways that merely enhance their characteristics. Some vegetables, on the other hand, inspire seemingly endless preparations; eggplant and artichokes are two that fall into that category, and either could fill a book of recipes. I've struggled to confine myself to a representative collection of some favorites, vegetable dishes that make regular appearances on my table.

Vegetables

If you come to Naples you will see Mount Vesuvius—and, most likely, me
on old magazine covers in a street stall.

Melanzane alla Parmigiana

EGGPLANT ALLA PARMIGIANA

With all my heart I believe that this is truly a glorious dish. But it's a dish with, for me, an impenetrable mystery. Why is it called alla Parmigiana, *referring to the people of the city of Parma, when it's as Neapolitan as Mount Vesuvius, and one of the proudest monuments of that city's gastronomy? Is it an injustice of history, an unwitting primal error, or some sinister plot hatched in high gastronomic circles?*

Provincial chauvinism aside, here's my way of preparing Eggplant alla Parmigiana.

FOR 4 SERVINGS

4 pounds eggplant

Salt

Extra-virgin olive oil

2 cloves garlic

1 pound canned peeled and crushed tomatoes

Fresh basil leaves

Freshly ground pepper

½ cup freshly grated Parmigiano cheese

1 pound fresh mozzarella, cubed

Cut the eggplant lengthwise into ½-inch slices. Layer the slices on a large plate and sprinkle each layer with salt. Place another plate of the same size on top of the pile of eggplant and place a heavy weight, such as a can of food, on the plate. Set aside to drain for 2 to 3 hours.

Meanwhile, heat about 2 tablespoons oil in a saucepan over medium heat and add the garlic. When it is lightly browned, add the tomatoes and basil; cook until the sauce is thick, then add salt and pepper to taste.

(continued)

Remove the weight from the eggplant, rinse the slices, and pat them dry. Generously cover the bottom of a large heavy skillet with olive oil and place it over high heat. Add the eggplant slices and brown them on both sides, adjusting the heat and adding oil as needed; you may have to cook the eggplant in more than one batch. Drain the slices on paper towels.

Preheat the oven to 350° F. Lightly coat an oblong (9-by-12-inch) ovenproof dish with tomato sauce. Arrange a layer of eggplant slices over the sauce and sprinkle them with the cheeses. Ladle a bit of the sauce over the cheeses, and then continue layering the ingredients until all are used up; you should end with sauce on top.

Bake for 15 to 20 minutes, to heat through and melt the mozzarella. Serve the *Melanzane alla Parmigiana* warm or at room temperature.

LEFT: *Just after the war, I am wearing a dress sent from relatives in America. The dress was a bit ridiculous, far from elegant, but in those days it seemed to me to be haute couture—"splendido!"*

ABOVE: *Another dress from America, modest and simple but very special to me.*

RIGHT: *Preparing* Melanzane alla Parmigiana *for the oven.*

Melanzane a Funghetto

EGGPLANT COOKED IN THE MANNER OF MUSHROOMS

Variations of this can be found all over Italy. It may be true that eggplant is far less scarce and expensive than mushrooms, but the appeal of Melanzane a Funghetto *is more than economical—it has all the charm of a culinary trompe-l'oeil.*

FOR 4 SERVINGS

2 small (1-pound) eggplants

Salt

3 to 4 tablespoons olive oil

2 to 3 cloves garlic, crushed

Freshly ground pepper

1 small tomato, peeled, seeded, and
    chopped (optional)

¼ cup chopped Italian parsley

Wash but do not peel the eggplants, then cut them lengthwise into quarters and cut away the center sections, removing most of the seeds. Cut the pieces crosswise into 1-inch chunks. Place the eggplant in a colander and sprinkle with salt. Let the eggplant drain for about 30 minutes, then pat them dry with paper towels.

Heat the oil in a large skillet over medium heat, add the garlic, and sauté briefly. Add the eggplant and cook slowly, stirring, over medium-high heat until the pieces are nicely crisped, about 15 minutes. Avoid the urge to add oil or the eggplant will not acquire the right mushroom-like texture. Adjust the heat as necessary to cook the eggplant thoroughly and at the same time crisp on the outside. Add the tomato and cook until the juices evaporate; season with salt and pepper to taste, stir in the parsley, and serve.

La Caponata

*C*aponata, *the delicious Sicilian specialty, can be defined as the quintessence of Mediterranean cuisine. In it you will find Greek, Arabic, and Spanish elements and flavors. It's uncertain how to categorize* La Caponata: *among antipasti; main dishes for lunch or light suppers; or, if you change the number to be served, as an accompaniment to main dishes. Versions of* caponata *are numerous, some are quite elaborate, but the results are always rewarding.*

For 4 to 6 Servings

---

4 small eggplants, 2 to 2½ pounds total

Olive oil

1 large onion, minced

1 cup tomato sauce such as *Salsa al Pomodoro Semplice* (page 61)

1 cup balsamic vinegar

12 black olives, pitted

2 stalks celery, diced

2 tablespoons drained capers

Salt

Freshly ground pepper

2 hard-boiled eggs, crumbled

Cut the eggplant into slices about 1 inch thick and sprinkle them with salt on both sides. Place the slices between sheets of paper towels and set aside for 4 hours. Pat the slices as dry as possible and cut them into cubes.

Pour about ½ inch oil into a large heavy skillet over medium-high heat. Add the eggplant and brown the cubes well—you may have to do this in more than one batch; add oil as needed. Drain the eggplant on paper towels.

Add the onion to the skillet; when it is lightly browned, add the tomato sauce. In a nonreactive saucepan, combine the vinegar, olives, celery, and capers and place over low heat. When the liquid is reduced by about a third, pour the mixture into the pan with the tomato sauce. Cook, stirring, until the tastes of the ingredients are blended well; season to taste with salt and pepper. Add the eggplant and cook over low heat for 15 minutes. Spoon the *caponata* onto a serving platter and let it cool to room temperature; top with the eggs. Cover and place the *caponata* in the refrigerator for a day before serving. Bring the *caponata* back to room temperature before serving.

Spiedini di Mozzarella e Melanzane

FRIED MOZZARELLA AND EGGPLANT ON SKEWERS

FOR **4** TO **6** SERVINGS

2 to 3 small eggplants, 2 to 2½ pounds total

Oil for frying

6 thick slices country-style or sturdy white bread

1 pound fresh mozzarella

12 or more small tomatoes or 3 to 4 medium tomatoes

4 eggs

Salt

Freshly ground pepper

Flour for dredging

Cut the eggplant into slices about 1½ inches thick. Pour about ½ inch of oil into a large heavy skillet and place over medium-high heat. When the oil is hot, fry the pieces of eggplant until nicely browned all over; add oil as needed. Drain the eggplant on paper towels.

Cut the eggplant slices, bread, mozzarella, and, if you are not using small ones, the tomatoes into cubes of roughly 1½ inches. Beginning with the bread, thread the bread, tomato, mozzarella, and eggplant onto skewers, continuing until the ingredients are used up.

In a large skillet heat a generous amount of oil. In a bowl large enough to hold the skewers, beat the eggs together with pinches of salt and pepper. Dredge the skewers in the flour and then dip them into the eggs. Dredge again, lightly, in the flour. Carefully place the skewers, a few at a time, into the hot oil and fry until golden brown all over. Serve immediately, while still very hot.

Torta di Patate

POTATO PIE

2 pounds potatoes, scrubbed

Salt

3 eggs

3 tablespoons unsalted butter

1 cup freshly grated pecorino cheese

3 ounces prosciutto, minced

2 tablespoons minced Italian parsley

Freshly ground pepper

Milk

Dry bread crumbs

½ pound fresh mozzarella or Italian fontina

Bring a large pot of water to a boil, add a pinch of salt, and drop in the potatoes. When the potatoes are soft and can easily be pierced with the tip of a sharp knife, drain them. When they are cool enough to handle, peel them.

Preheat the oven to 325° F.

Mash the potatoes, adding the eggs, 2 tablespoons butter, the pecorino, prosciutto, parsley, salt and pepper to taste, and as much milk as necessary to make a creamy, but not runny mixture.

Coat an oven-proof dish with some of the remaining butter and dust it with bread crumbs. Spoon half the potato mixture into the dish and smooth the top. Cut the mozzarella into thin slices and lay them over the potato mixture. Carefully spoon the remaining potato mixture over the cheese, sprinkle it lightly with additional bread crumbs, and dot with the remaining butter. Bake until heated through, about 30 minutes. Serve warm, rather than piping hot from the oven.

Purea di Patate

POTATO PURÉE

FOR 4 SERVINGS

---

2 pounds potatoes

1 cup light cream, warmed

3 tablespoons hot water

Salt

Wash and peel the potatoes and cut them into medium-sized chunks. Place the potatoes in a large pot, cover generously with cold water, and bring to a boil. When the potatoes are soft and can easily be pierced with the tip of a sharp knife, drain them and immediately pass them through a food mill or potato ricer into a saucepan. Over medium heat, add the cream while beating vigorously with a whisk until the potatoes are very fluffy; add the hot water and beat for another minute. Add salt to taste and serve at once.

Croquette di Patate

POTATO CROQUETTES

FOR 4 SERVINGS

2 pounds all-purpose potatoes

Salt

1 tablespoon butter

4 eggs

4 tablespoons all-purpose flour, plus additional for
   dredging

¼ teaspoon freshly ground nutmeg

2 cups dry bread crumbs

Oil for frying

Wash and peel the potatoes and cut them into medium-sized chunks. Place the potatoes in a large pot, cover generously with cold water, bring to a boil, and add a pinch of salt. When the potatoes are soft and can easily be pierced with the tip of a sharp knife, drain them and immediately pass them through a food mill or potato ricer into a bowl.

Melt the butter in a skillet over medium heat. Add the potatoes, 3 eggs, 4 tablespoons flour, and the nutmeg and whisk for about 1 minute. Turn the mixture out into a bowl and let it cool until it can be handled.

Flour a pastry board and your hands. In a small bowl whisk the remaining egg with 2 tablespoons water. Shape the potato mixture into logs about 4 inches long and 2 inches thick. Dredge the logs in the flour to coat them well, then into the beaten egg mixture, and finally, coat them with the bread crumbs.

Heat about 1 inch of oil in a large heavy skillet. When the oil is very hot, add the croquettes and fry them on both sides until they are golden brown all over. With a spatula, remove the croquettes to paper towels to drain briefly, and serve hot.

Mamma's Peperoni

MY MOTHER'S PEPPERS

I still remember with emotion the anticipation that overcame Mamma when I, by then married and with children of my own, would go to visit her in Rome. A few days together became a culinary festival for two, no guests, just she and I and so much conversation about whatever treats she brought to the table. In my memory those special days are a showcase of incomparable dishes—her Salsa Genovese, her Involtini di Vitello, and her roast peppers. For me it was a continuation of my education in cooking.

FOR 4 TO 5 SERVINGS

8 large or 10 medium plump yellow, red, and green
    bell peppers; look for smooth, wrinkle-free skin

4 tablespoons extra-virgin olive oil

3 cloves garlic, chopped

Salt

3 tablespoons freshly grated Parmigiano cheese

1½ tablespoons dry bread crumbs

Here I am at 2 years old, all dressed up for an outing with Mamma on Via Napoli, Pozzuoli's main street.

Roast the peppers whole in a very hot oven until the skin is charred on all sides. (Alternatively, do this directly over the flame of a gas burner, turning the peppers.) Remove the peppers from the oven and allow them to cool for a few minutes, until they can be handled. Carefully peel them, then remove the stems and seeds. Slice the peppers lengthwise into strips about ½ inch wide.

Heat the oil in a large skillet over medium heat, add the garlic, and sauté until golden. Add the pepper strips. Cook over medium heat for about 20 minutes, stirring gently once or twice. Add a pinch of salt, the cheese, and the bread crumbs. Stir for a minute or two, then serve.

It is not difficult to see why Mamma was the winner in a Greta Garbo look-alike contest.

MY MOTHER

At a year and a half, in the arms of my mother. This was a few years before the Second World War broke out and brought to our little town of Pozzuoli much misery, death, and difficulty; we were fortunate that our house remained unharmed by the bombs that fell frequently.

My mother also was an excellent cook but her artistic nature did not allow her to completely focus her energies on pots and pans. Her name was Romilda, a name my grandparents chose—who knows how?—from Handel's opera *Xerxes*, which is set in Persia. Mamma wore the name like her destiny and gave it an early test by choosing music as her vocation.

My mother's father was a poor metalworker more concerned with putting enough food on the table to feed many hungry mouths than with listening to the strains of the piano. Nevertheless, my mother managed to become an accomplished pianist. Besides talent, nature gave her extraordinary physical beauty, and this became both her glory and her burden. My father was her great love, but for her it was an unhappy and unfortunate love that gave her little joy. My sister, Maria, and I were the only light of that love.

A few years after we were born, with her beauty as her passport, Mamma received various offers to perform in film. She entered MGM's contest for the "Italian Garbo" and was the winner, but the timing was not right for a single mother of two little girls. As we grew up, it was in us that my mother invested all the hopes and ambitions that had been quashed in her. From when I was still quite young, Mamma dedicated herself to my success in film. This followed my own passion; I was a child who could spend hours in Pozzuoli's little movie theater, fascinated by Hollywood movie stars. Maria, on the other hand, had musical talent and followed that course.

It was in these early years of our childhood that Mamma took over from where Nonna Luisa had left off in the kitchen. Heredity cannot be denied, and I am indebted to her for a number of my own recipes, many little secrets, and much knowledge of food.

With my mother at home in Pozzuoli. I am about three years old and wearing my best Sunday dress. I also had a big bow in my hair that I thought looked like a butterfly— I adored it!

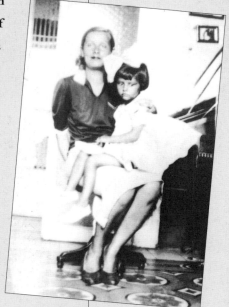

L'AGLIO: CROCE E DELIZIA

GARLIC: ITS BLESSING AND CURSE

*M*editerranean cuisine, which seems to have conquered the world, wouldn't exist as we know it without the characteristic presence of garlic. As for its "curse" I must address this other side of the coin: garlic has, along with its virtues, side effects that not everyone can tolerate. For some it is indigestion, for others it brings on a strong, harsh odor. You can tell, even from a distance, when someone has gone overboard with garlic, especially raw garlic.

Nevertheless there are several remedies for tolerating or dispelling the negative characteristics of this precious bulb. If handling garlic cloves directly while working with other ingredients, get yourself a pair of gloves—those thin plastic disposable ones—so that no bits become lodged under your nails or remain on the skin. If the recipe calls for minced garlic, cooking will soften its effect. There is another very simple solution, especially when garlic is an ingredient in sauces, pasta dishes, or soups. Those who cannot digest or tolerate garlic can add it to the pot, whole or lightly crushed, and then remove it at the very end of cooking, before the dish is served.

Spinaci del Monaco

THE MONK'S SPINACH

This recipe owes its name to its poor and humble ingredients. To tell the truth, I don't know if it is traditionally prepared in monasteries, but I like the name, especially since it is quick to prepare and costs little at the market. The recipe calls for spinach, but it is equally successful with other greens such as chard, escarole, and broccoli di rape.

FOR 4 TO 6 SERVINGS

4 pounds spinach

4 tablespoons extra-virgin olive oil

4 cloves garlic, crushed

Salt

Freshly ground pepper

Additional extra-virgin olive oil (optional)

Pick over the spinach, trim away all the tough stems, and wash it well. Place the spinach in a large pot or skillet over high heat, cover, and let it steam quickly in the water that is clinging to the leaves. Drain well, refresh under cold water, and pat dry with paper towels to absorb as much excess moisture as possible.

Heat the oil in a large shallow skillet; add the garlic and cook it over medium heat until it is lightly browned. Add the spinach and let it cook for a few minutes, turning it with a wooden spoon to absorb the flavors, then add salt and pepper to taste. A thin ribbon of your best olive oil can be added to each serving at the table.

Carciofi alla Giudia

ARTICHOKES, JEWISH STYLE

This is an extraordinary and excellent way to prepare artichokes. In the Jewish quarter of Rome, Carciofi alla Giudia is a specialty that has inspired keen competition among various restaurants, and many of them execute the dish exceedingly well. Giudia in Roman dialect means Jewish or Hebrew. The name of this brilliant dish derives more from the fact that it was born in the kitchens and restaurants of the city's picturesque neighborhood than from any Middle Eastern origins.

I must confess that I have prepared this dish many times, as has my sister, but our efforts always fall a little short of our expectations. If you want to taste the real Jewish-style artichokes, you must go to one of the restaurants in the old Roman quarter. In the meantime, with care, you can produce a pretty reasonable version in a home kitchen. Carciofi alla Giudia can be served as a separate course, and are especially good as an antipasto.

FOR 6 SERVINGS

---

12 round, medium-sized, very fresh, compact, and
    fleshy artichokes

Olive oil

Coarse salt

Freshly ground pepper

Remove the tough outer leaves of the artichokes. Next, cut off the tips without fear of taking off too much—you want only the tender, light-colored part of the leaves, and none of the dark green; pare away the tough, outer part of the stem and trim the underside of the base.

Hold the artichokes by the stem and push them down onto your work surface to open them and separate the leaves. Or, if the stems have been cut quite close to the head, place the artichokes against a flat surface, and gently press down until they open.

Heat about 1½ inches of oil in a large heavy pan over high heat. When the oil is very hot, place the artichokes, head down, into the oil and cook them for 5 minutes. Turn the artichokes over and cook for 5 minutes more. Continue cooking and turning until they are tender at the thickest part of their bottoms when pierced with a sharp knife. Turn them top down again, raise the heat to maximum, and cook for 1 final minute; the artichokes will become crisp, and will resemble a dried flower. Drain the artichokes on paper towels briefly, season to taste with salt and pepper, and serve them immediately.

Carciofi alla Romana

STUFFED ARTICHOKES, ROMAN STYLE

Although I adore Carciofi alla Giudia, I think this is my favorite, especially to prepare at home. Like many Italian vegetable dishes, this can be served as antipasto, or, cut into pieces, as a side dish or part of a mixed vegetable antipasto; serve them warm or at room temperature. Look for artichokes with compact heads and few tough, brown leaves.

FOR 6 SERVINGS

1 lemon

6 medium-sized artichokes

2 cloves garlic, chopped

2 tablespoons chopped fresh mint

1½ cups soft white bread crumbs

8 tablespoons olive oil

Salt

Freshly ground pepper

Squeeze the juice of the lemon into a large bowl and drop in the rinds; fill the bowl about halfway with cold water. Remove the tough outer leaves of the artichokes and trim the stem ends so that they are flat. With scissors, clip away the tips of the remaining leaves. As you prepare them, place the artichokes in the acidulated water.

Preheat the oven to 325° F.

In a mixing bowl, combine the garlic, mint, bread crumbs, 2 to 3 tablespoons oil, and salt and pepper to taste. Remove the artichokes from the bowl and shake out as much excess water as possible. Open the leaves of the artichokes. If you wish, the hairy choke can be removed from the centers using a spoon (or grapefruit spoon). In any case, divide the filling among them, spooning most of it deep into the centers and a bit into the outlying leaves.

Place the artichokes upright in a deep baking dish just large enough to hold them snugly and fill the dish with water to come about halfway up the artichokes. Drizzle the remaining oil over the artichokes and sprinkle them with salt and pepper. Cover the dish with foil and bake for about 1 hour, basting them with the pan juices from time to time. The artichokes are done when a leaf comes away with just a gentle tug.

THE NATURAL WAY

*I*n my kitchen, you'll find natural foods, but I'd like to say a thing or two about the word *natural*—in Italian, *genuino*. By natural, I mean a product straight from the source—the garden, the orchard, the butcher, the fishmonger, the herb market. I've nothing against packaged or frozen foods, but for me, nothing compares to a close encounter with food fresh from where it was grown or raised. When I'm in the States I go to a small outdoor market near my neighborhood every Thursday to shop for the week. How can I resist those beautifully fleshy red, yellow, and green peppers, sparklingly green broccoli, royal purple eggplant, those artichokes and pearly spring onions, the freshly picked fruit—plump cherries, tender apricots and peaches, succulent melons, fresh oranges—and so many greens, from spinach to arugula, lettuces, and the fresh herbs—basil, sage, and rosemary? Even humble parsley has more fragrance and flavor straight from the earth. These to me are the real natural foods, because they begin in one's mind, one's eyes, and end up on the stove and on the table.

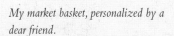

My market basket, personalized by a dear friend.

Indivia con Acciughe

ENDIVE AND ANCHOVIES

FOR 6 SERVINGS

6 large heads Belgian endive

Salt

2 tablespoons olive oil

2 cloves garlic, crushed, but left in one piece

3 to 4 anchovy fillets, drained and minced

Freshly ground pepper

10 to 12 fresh mint or parsley leaves

Bring a large pot of water to a boil. Trim the endive of any browned or broken leaves and wash away any dirt. Add a pinch of salt to the boiling water and drop in the endive; lower the heat to maintain a low boil, and cook for about 8 minutes; take care that the endive heads do not get soft. Drain and carefully refresh them under cold water.

When they are cool enough to handle, cut the endive heads in half lengthwise and lay them, face down, on paper towels. Heat the olive oil in a skillet large enough to hold the endive in one layer, and add the garlic cloves. Cook over medium heat until the garlic is golden brown, then remove and discard the garlic. Add the anchovies to the skillet and cook, stirring, until they disintegrate in the oil. Place the endive halves, face down, in the skillet and cook until they are golden, about 5 minutes. Gently turn the endive over, add the mint leaves to the pan, season to taste with pepper, and cook for 2 minutes longer. Serve hot.

LA CUCINA "SFIZIOSA"

THE WHIMSY KITCHEN

*S*tanding at the stove, seeking to be original and creative, brings on the urge to find a new dish, method, or combination that may be hidden within established recipes. That's how the whimsy kitchen is born. It's not by chance that I want to share with you this colorful Neapolitan word. *Sfizioso* is that little extra touch that takes a dish beyond its traditional form and adds a hint of fancy, sparking the curiosity and satisfying the most difficult palate.

Sfiziosi are the dishes that a wife prepares for her husband as a pleasant surprise; that a mother invents for her children with poor appetites; that are prepared in a hurry for the welcome but unexpected guest; those that have to stretch out a meager pantry without benefit of first-rate ingredients.

One dictionary defines the word *sfizio* as "a fanciful desire for something unimportant, but inspired by a fleeting mood." Another dictionary difines *sfizio* as "a fancy, a whim, fun." It goes without saying that this second definition is the one closest to my idea of *sfizio* in the kitchen.

LEFT: *Broccoli di rape prepared in the style of* Spinaci del Monaco *(page 169) is a good example of the* sfiziosa *approach, and demonstrates the flexibility of so many recipes.*
RIGHT: *Ingredients for* Scarola Riccia *(page 180).*

Scarola Riccia

STUFFED ESCAROLE

Believe it or not, these are often made as the filling of a covered pizza. This is a marvelous vegetable preparation on its own, one that can be served as an antipasto dish or as a side dish.

FOR 6 SERVINGS

6 small heads escarole

2 tablespoons chopped black olives

1 tablespoon pinoli

1 tablespoon drained capers

1 tablespoon olive oil, plus additional for cooking

Salt

Freshly ground pepper

If you can't find very small heads of escarole, get the smallest available and peel away the outer leaves; you will need one head for each serving. Wash the escarole thoroughly in a sinkful of water to remove any grit; drain.

In a small bowl combine the olives, pinoli, capers, 1 tablespoon oil, and salt and pepper to taste. Gently open the centers of each head of escarole and spoon in the stuffing, dividing it equally among them. Close the heads again and tie them with kitchen string to hold their shapes as they cook; wipe away any excess moisture.

Pour a generous amount of oil into a large heavy skillet and place it over medium-high heat. When the oil is hot, place the heads of escarole into the pan and brown them on all sides; don't overcrowd the pan—you may have to do this in two batches. When all the heads are nicely browned, place them in a serving dish, standing up if possible, and serve warm or at room temperature.

I've always liked the idea of making desserts with my own hands. It's a way of showing love and affection, perhaps more poetic than offering a gift or some frou-frou bought at a pastry shop. For me, working in the kitchen with sweet ingredients like vanilla, chocolate, and cream is relaxing and cheerful. Baking a cake or making a custard is not quite the same as preparing savory dishes; perhaps because it isn't done every day. The selection here consists of quite simple sweets, however, homey desserts like my Pan di Spagna, *not creations that demand the skills of an accomplished pastry chef.*

Desserts

*My career brought me much
more than I ever expected.
A Lifetime Achievement Oscar
was awarded to me in 1993.
To make the moment perfect,
the statuette was presented
by a very dear friend,
Gregory Peck.*

Quattro Quarti
POUND CAKE

FOR 8 SERVINGS

1⅛ cups sugar

1 cup unsalted butter, at room temperature

1 teaspoon grated orange zest

½ teaspoon vanilla extract

4 large eggs

1¾ cups all-purpose flour

2 teaspoons baking powder

½ cup plain yogurt

Preheat the oven to 350° F. Butter and flour a 10-inch cake pan.

Combine the sugar, butter, zest, and vanilla in a large bowl and beat the mixture until it is fluffy. In a separate mixing bowl, beat the eggs until they are light and foamy. Gradually combine the eggs with the sugar mixture.

Sift the flour and the baking powder into the mixture, stirring carefully to incorporate with a wooden spoon. Pour the batter into the pan and smooth the top with a spatula. Bake for 35 to 40 minutes, until the top is golden and a toothpick inserted in the center comes out clean. Remove the cake from the oven, let it rest for 1 minute, then turn it out onto a cake rack to cool.

I went to Spain to shoot The Pride and the Passion *with Frank Sinatra and Cary Grant. It was my first film for a Hollywood studio and I was intimidated to be working with two legendary actors. But from the beginning they were dear, generous colleagues.*

Pan di Spagna

SPONGE CAKE

The reasons for calling this cake "bread of Spain" have long since been lost in the mists of time. In any case, it is one of the cornerstones of Italian dessert-making, a cake that is fine just as it is, an example of the charm of simple things. It also is used in far more elaborate layer cakes and fancy "bombe," dome-shaped cakes that are filled with custards or ice cream.

FOR 8 SERVINGS

1 scant cup sugar

6 large egg yolks

2 teaspoons vanilla extract

6 large egg whites

1⅛ cups all-purpose flour, sifted

Butter for the pan

Heat the oven to 350° F. Butter and lightly flour a 10-inch cake pan, turning it upside down and tapping to let the excess flour fall off.

In a mixing bowl, beat the sugar and the egg yolks together until they are very pale in color; mix in the vanilla. In a separate bowl beat the egg whites to stiff peaks. Delicately fold the whites into the egg mixture, turning it over from the bottom to the top. Continuing to fold, sprinkle the flour over the mixture. When the flour is incorporated, gently pour the batter into the cake pan. Bake for about 40 minutes, or until the cake is golden and has begun to pull away from the sides of the pan. Remove the cake from the oven and place it on a rack to cool for 15 minutes, then turn it out onto the rack to cool completely.

Pastiera

WHEAT BERRY PIE

*W*heat, *so essential to bread and well-being, has always seemed practically sacred to me. Until recently, especially in large cities, it has been difficult, if not impossible, to find whole grain, or wheat berries. However, they seem to be enjoying new popularity, thanks to their wide appeal; they are healthful and flexible in dishes ranging from salad and soup to dessert. La Pastiera is a typical Neapolitan sweet, and there is no table, rich or poor, that doesn't boast its fine pastiera at Easter time.*

When I'm able to spend Easter in Rome, a very dear friend invariably dissuades me from buying pastiera for the Easter meal, promising to see to it himself. His secret is a tiny pastry shop near the Coliseum where everything is produced from scratch and the best pastiera in the world is made.

I feel I must warn you that pastiera takes some time to make because the wheat berries must be soaked and slowly cooked in advance. Otherwise, it will not strain the abilities of most home cooks. Since it is even better after a day, you can begin the preparation two days in advance.

FOR 8 TO 10 SERVINGS

FOR THE FILLING

½ pound (1 cup) wheat berries (available at health food stores and specialty food shops)

6 cups milk

¼ teaspoon vanilla extract

¼ teaspoon ground cinnamon

Zest of 1 orange (or lemon), finely minced

¾ pound fresh ricotta

8 ounces candied citron (*cedro*), finely minced

4 eggs, separated

1½ cups sugar

2 ounces orange-flower water

Butter for the pie plate

FOR THE PASTRY

   2¼ cups all-purpose flour

   Scant ¾ cup sugar

   1 cup vegetable shortening

   3 egg yolks

TO FINISH

   Powdered sugar

Twenty-four hours prior to preparation, rinse the wheat berries well, place them in a large bowl, and cover them generously with water. Soak the wheat berries for 2 hours. Drain them and put them into a large pot with the milk and 4 cups water over low heat. Bring the milk mixture to a simmer, cover, and cook until the wheat berries are tender and the liquid absorbed, which may be as long as 4 hours; add additional water if necessary.

When the wheat is cooked, stir in the vanilla, cinnamon, and zest. Let the mixture rest overnight in the refrigerator.

The following day, prepare a rich pie crust. Combine the flour and sugar and cut in the shortening and egg yolks. Divide the dough into two pieces, one slightly larger than the other, wrap them in plastic wrap, and refrigerate for about 1 hour.

In a large bowl blend the ricotta, 4 egg yolks, the candied citron, and the orange-flower water until the mixture is creamy. Stir in the wheat berry mixture and the sugar and blend well. In a separate bowl beat the egg whites to stiff peaks and fold them thoroughly into the mixture.

Preheat the oven to 350° F.

Generously butter a 10-inch pie plate. Roll out the larger piece of pie dough to a circle about 14 inches in diameter and fit it into the pie plate, letting the excess dough drape over the edge. Pour the ricotta mixture into the shell and smooth the top. Roll the second piece of dough into a rectangle and cut it into strips about 1 inch wide; cover the filling with the strips, creating a lattice pattern. Fold the edge of the dough over the strips and gently crimp them together. Bake for 30 to 40 minutes, until the pastry is golden and a knife inserted into the filling comes out clean. Let the pie cool to room temperature. Dust with powdered sugar before serving.

Torta di Ricotta

RICOTTA PIE

You can adjust the amounts of candied fruit and raisins according to your prefer-ence. If you use less fruit, you may want to increase the amount of sugar slightly to make up for their sweetness. You can also include the grated zest of an orange.

FOR 8 TO 10 SERVINGS

FOR THE PASTRY

  2 cups sifted all-purpose flour

  ½ cup sugar

  Large pinch salt

  8 tablespoons cold unsalted butter, cut into
    small pieces, plus additional for the pie plate

  1 whole egg

  1 egg yolk

  ¼ teaspoon grated lemon zest

FOR THE FILLING

  1 pound fresh ricotta

  ½ cup sugar

  1 whole egg

  2 egg yolks

  2 tablespoons white raisins

  1 tablespoon grated lemon zest

  1 tablespoon minced candie orange

  1 tablespoon minced candied
    citron (*cedro*)

  2 tablespoons pinoli

TO FINISH

  1 egg yolk

(continued)

To make the pastry, combine the dry ingredients in a bowl. Add the butter, and, with a fork or your fingers, work it in until the mixture is the consistency of coarse meal. In a small bowl beat the egg and yolk lightly, stir in the lemon zest, and pour it into the flour mixture. Using a fork or your fingers, mix to combine everything well and form the dough into two balls, one slightly larger than the other. If necessary, add a few tablespoons of iced water to hold the dough together.

Wrap the balls of dough in plastic wrap and let them rest in the refrigerator for 1 hour.

To make the filling, mix together the ricotta, sugar, egg, and yolks until they are well combined. Fold in the raisins, lemon zest, candied orange, candied citron, and the pinoli.

Preheat the oven to 350° F. Butter a 9-inch pie plate or a tart tin with a removable bottom.

Remove the larger ball of dough from the refrigerator and place it on a lightly floured work surface. Sprinkle the dough and your rolling pin with a bit of flour. Working from the center out in all directions, roll the dough into a circle 12 or so inches in diameter. Carefully line the pie plate or tart tin with the dough, letting the extra hang over the edge. This is a very "short" dough that may crumble, but don't be concerned—you can push or patch the dough together as necessary.

Pour the filling into the shell and smooth it with a spatula. Place the pie plate in the refrigerator or freezer while you roll out the second piece of dough. Place the dough on the work surface, flour it and the rolling pin, and roll it into a rectangle roughly 9-by-11 inches. With a knife or serrated ravioli cutter, cut the dough into strips about ½ inch wide. Cover the filling with the strips, creating a lattice pattern. Fold the edge of the bottom circle of dough over the strips and gently crimp them together.

Whisk the remaining egg yolk together with 1 teaspoon water. Brush the top of the dough, including the edge, with the egg mixture, taking care not to get it onto the filling.

Bake for 40 to 45 minutes, until the crust is golden brown and the filling is lightly colored. (The filling most likely will puff up, somewhat like a soufflé, but will collapse again.) Cool the pie on a rack. If you have used a tart tin, cool the pie on a rack for about 10 minutes, then remove the ring and continue to cool. Serve the pie at room temperature.

Tiramisù

PICK-ME-UP

$\mathcal{T}$*he name says it all:* Tirami-sù *means "pick me up." It means that if you're feeling down, list-less, in a negative mood, turning to this dessert will lighten your spirits, if not your body. My sons don't need this kind of help, but they do enjoy tremendously this simple version of tiramisù that Ines Bruscia, my devoted Italian secretary in Los Angeles, puts together.*

FOR 8 SERVINGS

3 eggs, separated

5 tablespoons sugar

6 ounces mascarpone cheese

1 to 2 packages ladyfingers (about 36; see Note)

1 cup orange liqueur such as Grand Marnier

1 cup espresso coffee

2 ounces bitter chocolate, grated

Scant ½ cup unsweetened cocoa powder or 2 ounces
grated bittersweet chocolate

Combine the egg yolks and sugar in a medium-sized bowl and beat them well. In a separate bowl, beat the egg whites to stiff peaks. In a third, larger bowl, combine the egg yolk mixture with the mascarpone, then fold in the egg whites to produce a creamy mixture.

Arrange a tight layer of ladyfingers in a 9-by-12-inch serving dish. Using a spoon, drizzle about half the liqueur and half the espresso over the ladyfingers. Cover the ladyfingers with the mascarpone mixture and the grated chocolate, and dust it with a little more than half the cocoa. Cover the filling with a second layer of ladyfingers and drizzle with the remaining liqueur and espresso. Place the dish in the refrigerator for at least 12 hours (the *tiramisù* can be made 24 hours in advance). Top with the remaining cocoa before serving.

NOTE: Found in specialty markets, as "Savoiardi" and often labeled for making *tiramisù*.

Crema Pasticciera

PASTRY CREAM

This custard sauce is delicious as the base of a fruit tart, alongside a simple cake like my Pan di Spagna *(page 186), or as a lovely accompaniment to fresh fruit, berries in particular.*

FOR **6** TO **8** SERVINGS

2 cups milk

1½ teaspoons vanilla extract

6 egg yolks

1 scant cup sugar

4 tablespoons sifted all-purpose flour

In a saucepan over medium-high heat, bring the milk just to the boiling point, add the vanilla, and remove from the heat. In a large bowl beat the egg yolks together with the sugar until the mixture is pale yellow, then whisk in the flour. Continuing to whisk, very slowly pour the hot milk into the egg mixture.

Pour the mixture back into the saucepan, and, stirring constantly, bring it slowly to close to the boiling point, but do not let it boil, or the eggs will curdle and you will have a lumpy sauce. Remove from the heat, cool briefly, then place a piece of waxed paper on the surface of the sauce to prevent a skin from forming. Cool to room temperature, then refrigerate until ready to use.

Banane al Forno

BAKED BANANAS

This is an extremely easy dessert to make when there's no time for something more elaborate.

FOR 6 SERVINGS

6 ripe bananas

Juice of 1 orange

6 tablespoons sugar

4 tablespoons unsalted butter

Rum (optional)

Preheat the oven to 350° F.

Butter a baking dish large enough to hold the bananas in one layer. Cut the bananas in half lengthwise and place them in the dish. Pour over the orange juice, sprinkle with the sugar, and dot with the butter. Place the dish in the oven and bake for 5 to 6 minutes, or until the top is lightly browned and glazed. Sprinkle lightly with rum and serve the bananas warm or at room temperature.

Budino di Castagne

CHESTNUT PUDDING

FOR 8 SERVINGS

2 quarts milk

1 pound dried chestnuts (available in specialty food
shops and Italian markets)

1 teaspoon vanilla extract

Salt

¼ cup plus 2 tablespoons sugar

¾ cup finely chopped toasted almonds

1 cup heavy cream

1 cup heavy cream, whipped (optional)

Chopped candied fruit or shaved chocolate

Place the milk in a medium-sized saucepan and bring to a boil; add the chestnuts, vanilla, and a small pinch of salt and simmer, partially covered, until the chestnuts are soft, about 2 hours. Pass the chestnuts, along with their cooking liquid, through a food mill. Place this purée into a saucepan over medium heat. Stir in the sugar and almonds, and blend the mixture well; remove the pan from the heat. Stir in the cream and spoon the mixture into 8 (4-ounce) individual custard cups or other dessert dishes or a serving dish. Let the molds chill in the refrigerator for 2 hours or longer. Top with whipped cream and candied fruit or shaved chocolate before serving.

Zabaione

SWEET-MARSALA CUSTARD

Zabaione was born in the south—Marsala, the wine that gives the dish its distinctive taste is also the name of the Sicilian city at the center of most of its production. In the last decades, however, zabaione has become known throughout the country and beyond; elegant Italian restaurants all over the world include it on their dessert menus. This is fine on its own, warm or cool, wonderful with strawberries or with a slice or two of Pan di Spagna *(page 186). I like* zabaione *made with a pinch of cinnamon.*

FOR 6 SERVINGS

6 egg yolks
6 tablespoons sugar
½ cup sweet Marsala wine
Ground cinnamon (optional)

Pour water to a depth of about 2 inches into the bottom of a double boiler, place it over medium-high heat, and bring it to a simmer. Stir the egg yolks, sugar, and 1 scant tablespoon water together in the top of the double boiler. Keeping the water in the bottom at a slow simmer, continue to stir until the mixture is smooth. Stirring more vigorously, slowly pour in the Marsala. Using a whisk, beat the mixture until it is pale gold in color, and light and frothy in consistency. Beat in a pinch of cinnamon if you like.

Gelo di Anguria

WATERMELON SEMIFREDDO

This is a dessert typical of Palermo, the capital of Sicily. It falls somewhere between an eggless custard and ice cream. In Sicilian dialect, in which big red watermelons are called muluni *(melons), it's called* gelu 'i muluni.

When I was in Palermo filming The Voyage *with Richard Burton, gelo di anguria (or gelo di cocomero, another word for watermelon) became a kind of addiction for us. It's a dessert that combines the sweetness of its ingredients with a fragrance that's fresh, light, and absolutely unique. To get the recipe we entered the kitchen of one of the most renowned pastry shops in Palermo, and it was only our celebrity that convinced the chef to allow us to observe the preparation (it was so simple!) of this delicious dessert.*

At first, this dessert may seem more sinfully fattening than it is, since its deceptive creaminess is not due to the inclusion of eggs, milk, or cream.

FOR 6 TO 8 SERVINGS

1 or more small watermelons, weighing 5 to
  6 pounds total

4 to 6 tablespoons sugar (see Note)

2 tablespoons cornstarch (see Note)

¼ teaspoon vanilla extract

2 tablespoons diced candied fruit

2 tablespoons sweet chocolate, roughly
  chopped

A scene from The Voyage.

Scoop out the red flesh of the melon, avoiding any of the white near the rind. Pass the pulp through a strainer or food mill to remove the seeds. You should have about 4 cups of strained flesh.

Place the flesh into a large deep saucepan with the sugar and the cornstarch. Place the pan over medium heat and stir constantly until the mixture just reaches the boiling point; it will appear creamy.

Remove the pan from the heat and let the mixture cool to room temperature. Stir in the vanilla, candied fruit, and chocolate. Pour the mixture into a 2-quart ice-cream mold or 8 individual molds or custard cups. Place the mold in the freezer for 3 hours or longer, until it is cold and thick but not hard. (If you have one, you can also process the mixture in an ice cream machine, according to its manufacturer's directions.) The *gelo di anguria* is now ready to delight your palate.

NOTE: The quantity of sugar and of cornstarch are adjustable according to taste. More or less cornstarch will affect the mixture's thickness; similarly, the degree of sweetness can be adjusted according to your taste and the sweetness of the melon itself. Also, there are those who prefer to use bitter or bittersweet chocolate and much more candied fruit.

Index

(Page numbers in *italic* refer
to illustrations.)

Academy Awards, vi, *67, 184*
Acciuga, spaghetti con burro di, 64
Aglio, 168
Agnello:
    bella Napoli, 115
    al forno, 119, *120–21*
    ubriaco, 118
Al dente, 49
Amatrice-style bucatini, 65
Acciuga, indivia con, 176, *177*
Anchovy(ies):
    butter sauce, spaghetti with, 64
    endive and, 176, *177*
    pasta quills, whore style, 76
Anguria, gelo di, 200–201
Annibale (Rome), *98*
Antipasti and small dishes, 2–27
    asparagus pie, savory, 18, *18–19*
    caponata, 158–59, *159*
    escarole, stuffed, 180, *181*
    frittatas, 21
    grilled country bread (*bruschetta*), 10
    luxurious salad, *25,* 27
    mozzarella in carrozza, 6, *8–9*
    mozzarella and tomatoes, 10
    omelet, Neapolitan, 20
    panzanella, 24, *25*
    pizza, classic Neapolitan, *12,* 12–13
    pizza, country-style, 16
    pizzas, fried Neapolitan, *14,* 15, *15*
    polenta, toasted, 5, *8–9*
    prosciutto with figs, 7
    prosciutto with melon, 8, *8–9*
    white beans with caviar, 11
Aragosta al rum, 148
Artichokes:
    Jewish style, 170–71, *171*
    stuffed, Roman style, 172–73
Asparagi:
    risotto ai formaggio e, 84, *85*
    torta di, 18, *18–19*
Asparagus:
    pie, savory, 18, *18–19*
    risotto with cheese and, 84, *85*
Avena, minestra di, 44–45

Baccalà, 131–34
    ai ferri, 134
    in insalata, 132, *133*
    see also Salt cod
Bananas, baked, 196
Banane al forno, 196
Barthet, Jean, *109*
Basil, in *pesto genovese,* 72, *73*
Bass, Christmas, 140–41, *142–43, 145*
Bean(s):
    fava, soup, 40–41, *41*
    rice, and potato soup, 37
    minestrone, 32–33, *33*
    pasta e fagioli, 38
    with pork rind, 35–36
    white, with caviar, 11
Beef:
    carpaccio, 114
    Châteaubriand, grilled, 112–13, *113*
    meatballs, 111
    patties, 109–10
    rolls, stuffed, and sauce, Neapolitan, *56,* 57–58, *58*
Boccaccio '70, 122
Bread:
    country, grilled (*bruschetta*), 10
    panzanella, 24, *25*
Broccoli di rape, monk's, 169, *178*
Bruschetta, 10
Bucatini:
    in Amatrice style, 65
    alla carbonara, 66–68, *69*

Bucatini:
    all'amatriciani, 65
    alla carbonara, 66–68, *69*
Budino di castagne, 197
Burton, Richard, 200, *200*

Cakes:
    pound, 185
    sponge, 186, *187*
Capon, stuffed, in Emilia style, 124–25
Caponata, 158–59, *159*
Cappone emiliano, 124–25
Carciofi:
    alla giudia, 170–71, *171*
    alla romana, 172–73
Carne:
    piatto di, rustica, 104, *105*
    polpette di, 111
    timpano di pomodoro e, 52–53
Carpaccio, 114
Castagne, budino di, 197
Cauliflower, cold salt cod with, 132, *133*
Caviale, fagioli al, 11
Caviar, white beans with, 11
Châteaubriand, grilled, 112–13, *113*
Cheese:
    polenta with butter and, 95, *95*
    risotto with asparagus and, 84, *85*
Chestnut pudding, 197
Chicken roasted as pork, 122–23, *123*
Christmas bass, 140–41, *142–43*, *145*
Clams, spaghetti with, 77
Cod, salt. *See* Salt cod
Coniglio alle erbe, 126, *127*
Cotiche:
    fagioli con le, 35–36
    minestra di farro e, 42–43
Count's rice, 86–87
Crema pasticciera, 194, *195*
Croquette di patate, 163
Croquettes, potato, 163
Crostini, polenta, 5, *8–9*
Custard, sweet-Marsala, 198, *199*

Da Michele (Naples), *17*
De Filippo, Eduardo, 59
De Sica, Vittorio, 11, 59, 66, *67*
Desserts, 182–201
    bananas, baked, 196
    chestnut pudding, 197
    pastry cream, *194*, 195
    pick-me-up (*tiramisù*), 193
    pound cake, 185
    ricotta pie, *190–91*, 190–92
    sponge cake, 186, *187*
    sweet-Marsala custard, 198, *199*
    watermelon semifreddo, 200–201
    wheat berry pie, 188–89
Drunken lamb, 118

Eggplant:
    caponata, 158–59, *159*
    cooked in manner of mushrooms, 157
    fried mozzarella and, on skewers, 160
    alla parmigiana, 153–54, *155*
Eggs:
    frittatas, 21
    luxurious salad, *25*, 27
    omelet, Neapolitan, 20
Eisenstaedt, Alfred, *103*
Emilia-Romagna, dishes from
    stuffed capon, 124–25
    chicken roasted as pork, 122–23, *123*
Endive and anchovies, 176, *177*
Escarole, stuffed, 180, *181*

Fagioli:
    al caviale, 11
    con le cotiche, 35–36
    minestra di riso, patate e, 37
    pasta e, 38
Farro, minestra di cotiche e, 42–43
Farro soup with *cotiche*, 42–43
Fava bean soup, 40–41, *41*
Fave, minestra di, 40–41, *41*
Fichi al prosciutto, 7
Figs, prosciutto with, 7
Filetto alla griglia, 112–13, *113*

First courses. See Pasta; Polenta; Risotto
Fish and shellfish, 128–48
    bass, Christmas, 140–41, *142–43*, *145*
    flamed roast fish, 139
    grilled seafood on skewers, 147, *147*
    lobster with rum, 148
    salt cod, grilled, 134
    salt cod with cauliflower, cold, 132, *133*
    sardines, stuffed, 138
    sole, fillet of, in Marsala sauce, *136*, 137
    tuna, fresh, with mushrooms, 135
Formaggio, risotto ai asparagi e, 84, *85*
Fried dishes:
    mozzarella and eggplant on skewers, 160
    pizzas, Neapolitan, *14*, 15, *15*
Frittatas, 21
Frittate, 21
Funghi:
    risotto ai, 88–89
    tonno fresco con , 135

Gable, Clark, *81*
Garlic, 168
Gelo di anguria, 200–201
Gorgonzola, pasta con crema di, 60–61
Gorgonzola cream, pasta with, 60–61
Grant, Cary, *185*
Grilled dishes:
    Châteaubriand, 112–13, *113*
    country bread (*bruschetta*), 10
    fish, flamed roast, 139
    lobster with rum, 148
    salt cod, 134
    seafood on skewers, 147, *147*

Harry's Bar (Venice), 114

Indivia con acciuga, 176, *177*
Insalata ricca, 25, 27
It Started in Naples, *80*, *81*

Jewish-style artichokes, 170–71, *171*

Lamb:
    from beautiful Naples, 115
    drunken, 118
    roasted leg of, 119, *120–21*
Lemon, spaghetti with, 75
Lenticchie:
    risotto con, 90, *91*
    zuppa di, 31
Lentil(s):
    soup, 31
    risotto with, 90, *91*
Limone, spaghetti al, 75
Linguine con salsa Sophia, 70–71, *71*
Linguine with Sophia's sauce, 70–71, *71*
Lobster with rum, 148
Loren, Sophia, photos of, *vi, 4, 13, 26, 39, 48, 67, 77, 108,*
    134, 139, 146, 152, 154, 172, 173, 184
    as child, *xi, 102, 103, 165, 167*
    film stills, *34, 35, 59, 66, 80, 81, 122, 149, 185, 200*
Lunch or supper dishes:
    asparagus pie, savory, 18, *18–19*
    caponata, 158–59, *159*
    frittatas, 21
    omelet, Neapolitan, 20
    panzanella, 24, *25*
Luxurious salad, *25*, 27

Maionese, 144
Marriage Italian Style, *34*, 59
Marsala:
    sauce, fillet of sole in, *136*, 137
    sweet-, custard, 198, *199*
Mastroianni, Marcello, 11, *11*, *34*, 35, *35*, 59
Mayonnaise, 144
Meat, 96–127
    pasta with tomatoes and, baked, 52–53
    patties, 109–10
    see also Beef; Lamb; Veal
Meatballs, 111
Melanzane:
    a funghetto, 157
    alla parmigiana, 153–54, *155*
    spiedini di mozzarella e, 160
Melon, prosciutto with, 8, *8–9*

Melone e prosciutto, 8, *8–9*
Minestre:
    di avena, 44–45
    di farro e cotiche, 42–43
    di fave, 40–41, *41*
    di riso, patate, e fagioli, 37
Minestrone, 32–33, *33*
Monk's spinach, 169
Mozzarella:
    in carrozza, 6, *8–9*
    fried eggplant and, on skewers, 160
    and tomatoes, 10
Mozzarella:
    in carrozza, 6, *8–9*
    e pomodori, 10
    spiedini di melanzane e, 160
Mushroom(s):
    fresh tuna with, 135
    risotto, 88–89

Naples, *17, 42, 54–55, 116–17, 130*
Natural foods, 174
Neapolitan dishes:
    eggplant *alla parmigiana*, 153–54, *155*
    lamb from beautiful Naples, 115
    omelet, 20
    pizza, classic, *12*, 12–13
    pizzas, fried, *14*, 15, *15*
    stuffed beef rolls and sauce, *56*, 57–58, *58*

Oat soup, 44
Olives:
    luxurious salad, *25*, 27
    pasta quills, whore style, 76
Omelet, Neapolitan, 20
Omelet napoletana, 20

Pan di Spagna, 186, *187*
Panzanella, 24, *25*
Parmigiano:
    eggplant *alla parmigiana*, 153–54, *155*
    polenta with, 94
Parsley, in linguine with Sophia's sauce, 70–71, *71*

Pasta, 46–77
    bucatini in Amatrice style, 65
    bucatini alla carbonara, 66–68, *69*
    buying, 49
    cooking, 49
    dough, fresh, 51
    e fagioli, 38
    fresh, 50
    with Gorgonzola cream, 60–61
    linguine with Sophia's sauce, 70–71, *71*
    with meat and tomatoes, baked, 52–53
    quills, whore style, 76
    shapes of, 50
    spaghetti with anchovy butter sauce, 64
    spaghetti with basic tomato sauce, 61
    spaghetti with clams, 77
    spaghetti with lemon, 75
    spaghetti with uncooked tomato sauce, 62, *63*
    stuffed beef rolls and sauce, Neapolitan, *56*, 57–58,
        58
    tagliatelle with zucchini, 74
    trenette con pesto
genovese, 72, *73*
Pasta:
    bucatini all'amatriciani, 65
    bucatini alla carbonara, 66–68, *69*
    con crema di Gorgonzola, 60–61
    e fagioli, 38
    linguine con salsa Sophia, 70–71, *71*
    penne alla puttanesca, 76
    ragù alla napoletana, *56*, 57–58, *58*
    spaghetti con burro di acciuga, 64
    spaghetti al limone, 75
    spaghetti con pomodoro crudo, 62, *63*
    spaghetti con salsa al
pomodoro semplice, 61
    spaghetti con vongole, 77
    tagliatelle con zucchini, 74
    timpano di carne e
pomodoro, 52–53
    trenette con pesto genovese, 72, *73*
Pastiera, 188–89
Pastry cream, *194*, 195
Patate:

croquette di, 163
minestra di riso, fagioli e, 37
purea di, 162
torta di, 161
Peas, risotto with, 82
Peck, Gregory, 184
Penne alla puttanesca, 76
Peperoni, Mamma's, 164, 165
Peppers, my mother's, 164, 165
Pesto genovese, trenette con, 72, 73
Piatto di carne rustica, 104, 105
Piazza del Plebiscito (Naples), 116–17
Piccatina di vitello, 105, 107
Pick-me-up (tiramisù), 193
Pies (savory):
    asparagus, 18, 18–19
    potato, 161
Pies (sweet):
    ricotta, 190–91, 190–92
    wheat berry, 188–89
Piselli, risotto con, 82
Pizza(s):
    classic Neapolitan, 12, 12–13
    country-style, 16
    fried Neapolitan, 14, 15, 15
Pizza rustica, 16
Polenta, 93–95
    basics, 93–94
    with butter and cheese, 95, 95
    microwave method, 94
    with Parmigiano, 94
    toasted, 5, 8–9
Polenta:
    crostini, 5, 8–9
    al parmigiano, 94–95
    pasticciata, 95, 95
Pollo alla porchetta, 122–23, 123
Polpette:
    di carne, 111
    di Livia, 109–10
Pomodoro(i):
    crudo, spaghetti con, 62, 63
    mozzarella e, 10
    spaghetti con salsa al,

semplice, 61
    timpano di carne e, 52–53
Ponti, Carlo (husband), 108
Ponti, Carlo, Jr. (son), 11, 108–10, 109
Ponti, Edoardo (son), 108–10, 109
Pork rind (cotiche):
    beans with, 35–36
    farro soup with, 42–43
Potato(es):
    croquettes, 163
    luxurious salad, 25, 27
    pie, 161
    purée, 162
    rice, and bean soup, 37
Pound cake, 185
Pride and the Passion, The, 185
Prosciutto:
    with figs, 7
    with melon, 8, 8–9
    sautéed veal with sage and, 105, 106
Prosciutto:
    fichi al, 7
    melone e, 8, 8–9
Pudding, chestnut, 197
Purea di patate, 162

Quattro quarti, 185

Rabbit with herbs, 126, 127
Ragù alla napoletana, 56, 57–58, 58
Rice, 78–92
    Count's, 86–87
    potato, and bean soup, 37
Ricotta, torta di, 190–91, 190–92
Ricotta pie, 190–91, 190–92
Riso:
    del conte, 86–87
    minestra di patate, fagioli e, 37
Risotto, 81–92
    with asparagus and cheese, 84, 85
    basics, 81
    from Geneva, 83
    with lentils, 90, 91
    mushroom, 88–89

with peas, 82
saffron-flavored, 92
Risotto:
    ai asparagi e formaggio, 84, *85*
    ai funghi, 88–89
    di Ginevra, 83
    con lenticchie, 90, *91*
    alla milanese, 92
    con piselli, 82
Roman-style stuffed artichokes, 172–73
Rome, *98*, *124*

Saffron-flavored risotto, 92
Salad, luxurious, *25*, 27
Salt cod (*baccalà*), 131–34
    basics, 131
    with cauliflower, cold, 132, *133*
    grilled, 134
Saltimbocca, 105, *106*
Sardines, stuffed, 138
Sardines a beccafico, 138
Saturday, Sunday and Monday, 59
Sauces:
    pesto genovese, 72, *73*
    ragù alla napoletana, *56*, 57–58, *58*
    salsa Sophia, 70–71, *71*
    tomato, basic, 61
    tomato, uncooked, 62, *63*
Scandal in Sorrento, 149
Scarola riccia, 180, *181*
Scicolone, Maria (sister), *102*, 103, *103*, 167
Second courses, 96–127
    capon, stuffed, in Emilia style, 124–25
    carpaccio, 114
    Châteaubriand, grilled, 112–13, *113*
    chicken roasted as pork, 122–23, *123*
    Count's rice, 86–87
    meatballs, 111
    meat patties, 109–10
    rabbit with herbs, 126, *127*
    see also Fish and shellfish; Lamb; Veal
Semifreddo, watermelon, 200–201
Sfiziosa approach, 178
Shellfish. *See* Fish and shellfish

Sicilian dishes:
    caponata, 158–59, *159*
    sardines, stuffed, 138
    watermelon semifreddo, 200–201
Sinatra, Frank, *185*
Sogliola, filetti di, con
 salsa all'uovo, *136*, 137
Sogno, *26*
Sole, fillet of, in Marsala sauce, *136*, 137
Soups, 28–45
    beans with pork rind, 35–36
    farro, with *cotiche*, 42–43
    fava bean, 40–41, *41*
    lentil, 31
    minestrone, 32–33, *33*
    oat, 44
    pasta e fagioli, 38
    rice, potato, and bean, 37
Spaghetti:
    with anchovy butter sauce, 64
    with basic tomato sauce, 61
    with clams, 77
    with lemon, 75
    with uncooked tomato sauce, 62, *63*
Spaghetti:
    con burro di acciuga, 64
    al limone, 75
    con pomodoro crudo, 62, *63*
    con salsa al pomodoro semplice, 61
    con vongole, 77
Special Day, A, 35
Spezzatino di vitello, 102
Spiedini:
    alla marinara, 147, *147*
    di mozzarella e melanzane, 160
Spigola di Natale, 140–41, *142–43*, *145*
Spinach, monk's, 169
Spinaci del monaco, 169
Sponge cake, 186, *187*
Sunflower, 11, *11*
Sweet-Marsala custard, 198, *199*

Tagliatelle con zucchini, 74
Tagliatelle with zucchini, 74

Tastuccio (Rome), *124*

Tempo, 152

Timpano di carne e pomodoro, 52–53

Tiramisù, 193

Tomato(es):

    mozzarella and, 10

    panzanella, 24, *25*

    pasta with meat and, baked, 52–53

    sauce, basic, spaghetti with, 61

    sauce, uncooked, spaghetti with, 62, *63*

Tonno fresco con funghi, 135

Torte:

    di asparagi, 18, *18–19*

    di patate, 161

    di ricotta, 190–91, *190–92*

Trenette con pesto genovese, 72, *73*

Tuna:

    fresh, with mushrooms, 135

    luxurious salad, *25,* 27

Turkey, in Count's rice, 86–87

Two Women, vi, 66, *66, 67*

Veal:

    cooked in manner of pizza chef, 100, *101*

    country-style, 104, *105*

    meatballs, 111

    patties, 109–10

    roast, 99

    sautéed, with lemon, *105,* 107

    sautéed, with prosciutto and sage, *105,* 106

    stew, 102

Vegetable dishes, 150–81

    artichokes, Jewish style, 170–71, *171*

    artichokes, stuffed, Roman style, 172–73

    caponata, 158–59, *159*

    eggplant cooked in manner of mushrooms, 157

    eggplant *alla parmigiana,* 153–54, *155*

    endive and anchovies, 176, *177*

    escarole, stuffed, 180, *181*

    mozzarella and eggplant on skewers, fried, 160

    peppers, my mother's, *164,* 165

    potato croquettes, 163

    potato pie, 161

    potato purée, 162

    spinach, monk's, 169

Vesuvius, *54–55*

Villani, Mario and Dora, *30*

Villani, Romilda (mother), *102,* 165, 166, 167, *167*

Vitello:

    arrosto, 99

    piccatina di, 105, 107

    alla pizzaiola, 100, *101*

    saltimbocca, 105, 106

    spezzatino di, 102

Volpetti, Claudio, *102*

Vongole, spaghetti con, 77

Voyage, The, 200, *200*

Watermelon semifreddo, 200–201

Watteville, Hubert, 109

Wheat berry pie, 188–89

White bean(s):

    with caviar, 11

    with pork rind, 35–36

    rice, and potato soup, 37

Zabaione, 198, *199*

Zucchini, tagliatelle con, 74

Zucchini, tagliatelle with, 74

Zuppa di lenticchie, 31

GREMESE

Gastronomy

Maria Chiara Martinelli
AL DENTE
208 pages, 129 colour photos
hardback US$ 29.95   GB£ 18.95
paperback US$ 19.95   GB£ 12.95

Paolo Scotto
WINE AND CHEESE OF ITALY
Two volume set of
148 pages, hardback,
200 colour photos,
32 colour maps,
21 recipes
US$ 29.95   GB£ 14.95

Jean François Dormoy – Frank Artigaud
WINE AND CHEESE OF FRANCE
Two volume set of 148 pages, hardback,
228 colour photos, 13 colour maps,
32 recipes
US$ 29.95   GB£ 14.95

Cinema

Stefano Masi –
Enrico Lancia
SOPHIA
192 pages, hardback,
263 b/w photos,
30 colour photos
US$ 29.95
GB£ 19.95

Claudio G. Fava
ALBERTO SORDI
An American in Rome
192 pages, hardback, 138 b/w photos
US$ 39.95   GB£ 19.95

Stefano Masi
ROBERTO BENIGNI
80 pages, paperback,
80 colour and b/w photos
US$ 12.95   GB£ 7.99

Silvia Bizio
CINEMA ITALIAN STYLE
Italians at the Academy Awards
Foreword by Bernardo Bertolucci
160 pages, paperback, 141 b/w photos
US$ 19.95   GB£ 12.95

Gilles Dagneau
AVA GARDNER
*Beautiful, Wild,
Innocent*
192 pages, hardback,
140 b/w photos,
30 colour photos
US$ 29.95   GB£ 19.95

Matilde Hochkofler
**MARCELLO
MASTROIANNI**
The Fun of Cinema
208 pages,
hardback,
190 b/w photos
US$ 29.95
GB£ 19.95

Jean A. Gili
ITALIAN FILMMAKERS
Self Portraits: A Selection of Interviews
192 pages, paperback, 100 b/w photos,
10 colour photos
US$ 24.95   GB£ 15.95

Oreste De Fornari
SERGIO LEONE
*The Great Italian Dream
of Legendary America*
184 pages, hardback, 150 b/w photos
US$ 39.95   GB£ 24.95

Lorenzo Cuccu
THE CINEMA OF PAOLO AND VITTORIO TAVIANI
*Nature, Culture and History Revealed by
Two Tuscan Masters*
224 pages, hardback, 100 b/w photos,
85 colour photos
US$ 29.95   GB£ 19.95

Stefano Masi – Enrico Lancia
ITALIAN MOVIE GODDESSES
*Over 80 of the Greatest Women
in Italian Cinema*
192 pages, hardback,
150 b/w photos
US$ 29.95   GB£ 19.95

Fabrizio Borin
FEDERICO FELLINI
*A Sentimental Journey
into the Illusion and the
Reality of a Genius*
192 pages, hardback,
130 b/w photos,
30 colour photos
US$ 29.95   GB£ 19.95

Other titles also available:
SILVANA MANGANO
PIETRO GERMI